INDIAN
Cook Book

PURBA SINGH

MEREHURST

Published in 1995 by Merehurst Limited
Ferry House, 51–57 Lacy Road, Putney, London SW15 1PR

Reprinted 1995, 1996

Copyright © 1995 Merehurst Limited

ISBN 1–85391–416–9

A catalogue record for this book is available from the
British Library

Series Editor: Valerie Barrett
Design: Clive Dorman
Illustrations: Keith Sparrow

Typeset by Clive Dorman & Co.
Colour Separation by P&W Graphics Pty Ltd, Singapore
Printed and bound in Great Britain by
Mackays of Chatham PLC, Chatham, Kent

RECIPE NOTES

 Indicates dishes that cook in under 35 minutes

- Follow one set of measurements only, do not mix metric and imperial
- All spoon measures are level
- Always taste and adjust seasonings to suit your own preferences

 Indicates dishes that are suitable for vegetarians

CONTENTS

INTRODUCTION

Indian restaurants and take-away food have been popular in this country for many years. Recently supermarkets have been selling many previously hard to get ethnic foods, and specialist food shops are also on the increase. This now makes it easy for anyone to cook their favourite Indian dishes at home.

One of the misconceptions about Indian food is that it is difficult to cook. A great mystique surrounds the grinding and mixing of spices, some of which are unfamiliar, and there is the fear that unless you get it absolutely right the flavour will be ruined. Well nothing could be further from the truth, Indian cookery does not need fancy equipment and is very flexible as there are few 'right or wrong ways' to do it. You can add more of a certain spice if you like it, or less if you don't, you can add other ingredients, make a dish thicker or thinner in consistency, it is up to you. There are many classic dishes such as Rogan Josh, or Tikka Masala, but as these recipes have been handed down through different families through history, no two Indian cooks will make them in exactly the same way. Start by using the recipes in this book and then as you get more familiar with tastes and textures, change them to suit yourself – less chilli if you don't like hot curries, more liquid if you like moist ones – you can develop your own version.

You will find all your favourites here, from Onion Bhajias to Pork Vindaloo, Lamb Korma, Chicken Biryani, Bhuna Prawns and many others. Also included are recipes reflecting the different regions of India, such as tandoori and Mogul dishes from the North, and dishes flavoured with coconut, tamarind, curry leaves and hot spices, from the South. India is a country of fasts and festivals so there are a couple of festive dishes such as Lamb Pullao and Rose-Scented Saffron Rice, which are very attractive and worth making for a special occasion. Every Indian meal is a feast in itself, so enjoy cooking and eating the Really Indian way.

EQUIPMENT

The nice thing about Indian cooking is that you don't have to go out and buy lots of new equipment or dishes. Most cooking can be done in ordinary frying pans, saucepans and casseroles. It is useful, but not essentia,l to have a wok, and if you do have one, it can double as a balti pan which is very similar. A barbecue is good to have in the summer for cooking some of the grilled recipes, but again not essential.

One thing that is useful if you want to grind your own spices, is a pestle and mortar or a small coffee grinder. The latter should be kept especially for spices, or you may end up with odd flavoured coffee. Food processors, blenders and mechanical vegetable choppers are very useful and time saving.

INGREDIENTS

Asafoetida

Sometimes called hing, this is a distinctive-smelling gum resin, which originates as the milky sap of a giant fennel plant. The smell disappears during cooking and it is used in very small quantities to flavour meat, fish, dhals and vegetable dishes. It comes in pieces (which then have to be ground) or powder form, and can be bought in Asian food shops.

Black Onion Seeds

They have a strong bittersweet flavour and are used for rice dishes, stir-fried vegetable dishes and as a topping for some breads. Find them in Asian stores, but if you have difficulty they can be omitted from a recipe.

Black Salt

This is rock salt that has traces of sulphur in it. It is spicy and extremely pungent and gives a very distinctive flavour even though it is used in small amounts. You can buy it in a piece, grind it yourself and keep in an airtight container, or buy it ready-ground. Available in Asian food stores.

Cardamom

The pleasant-scented flavour of cardamom is essential to many Indian dishes. There are two varieties of cardamom; the large type has a black pod and black seeds inside and is used for savoury dishes, in spice bags and as an ingredient for garam masala. The small type is green and used for pickles, pilaus and sweets and desserts. Cardamoms may be used whole, or ground, or the seeds only may be required. Ground cardamom is available in most supermarkets, but you may need to go to an Asian store to buy the whole pods.

Chilli

Fresh chillies are used in many Indian dishes and you can vary the amount you use to suit your own taste. Fresh chillies contain an irritant that causes painful stinging and swelling if you touch your eyes or mouth. When preparing chillies either wear rubber gloves or wash your hands thoroughly immediately afterwards.

Fresh green chillies – these give a distinctive hot taste to many dishes. The seeds are the hottest part and these may be discarded if you want a less fiery dish.

Fresh red chillies – these are available in several shapes and sizes, but a general rule is, the smaller, narrower and darker the chilli, the more pungent it is.

Dried chillies – both red and green are available in dried form and are used in pickles, spice bags and so on.

Chilli powder – this is available in most supermarkets in varying strengths and should be used sparingly to suit your own taste. It is not meant to mask other flavours.

Chilli Paste (Sambal Oelek)

Crushed fresh red chillies made into a paste. It is sold in jars in Oriental and Thai specialist shops, and larger supermarkets.

Coconut

Coconut and coconut milk are used for many Indian dishes. When a recipe calls for grated coconut the best flavour and texture will be obtained by using a fresh coconut. To use a fresh coconut, simply pierce one of the 'eyes' at the base of the coconut with a skewer or screwdriver and drain off the water. (This liquid is coconut water not milk.) Tap the coconut sharply in the middle with a hammer in order to make it split. With a sharp knife, prize away the white flesh. Peel off the brown skin and grate or slice the flesh according to the recipe. The coconut flesh can be frozen in small batches to use later. Desiccated coconut can be used instead, but make sure that you buy the unsweetened variety.

Coconut milk is also used a lot in curry dishes and can be obtained in several ways. Coconut milk can be bought in dried powder form or in cans, from larger supermarkets and Oriental and Asian stores. Creamed coconut, which is bought in blocks from supermarkets or health food shops, can be grated or chopped and heated gently with water to make coconut milk. Alternatively, you can make coconut milk as follows. Put 500 ml (16 fl oz) milk into a pan and bring to the boil. Remove from the heat and stir in 250g (8 oz) grated fresh or unsweetened desiccated coconut. Leave to become cold, then pour through a sieve, pressing with a spoon to extract as much liquid as possible. Use full cream milk for a rich result.

Coriander

One of the most important ingredients in Indian cooking, fresh green coriander is used as liberally as parsley is used in British dishes, especially for garnishing. The most economical place to buy fresh coriander is in Asian stores where it is sold in large bunches. The small beige coloured coriander seeds are used whole or more often in their ground form, and both types can be bought easily in supermarkets. Dried coriander is never a substitute for fresh coriander.

Cumin

These are caraway-like seeds and are used whole or ground. White cumin is easy to obtain and is used a great deal.

Black cumin is smaller and darker than the ordinary type and has a much stronger smell. It is not used so often as the white type, but when needed can be purchased in Asian food stores.

Curry Leaves

These are the green leaves of a tree found in India. They are used in a similar way to bay leaves, being added to a dish for flavouring and removed just before serving. Both green and dry leaves are available from Asian stores.

Fennel Seeds

Similar to white cumin seeds, they are used whole or ground and give a tangy minty flavour.

Fenugreek

Fenugreek seeds are small, dark orange and rectangular and have a bittersweet taste. They can be used whole or in ground form. Fenugreek leaves can be bought fresh or dried from some Asian stores and can be used as a herb for flavouring.

Garam Masala

The name means 'mixed spice' and it is a mixture of spices which is sprinkled over a finished dish or added during cooking, often towards the end. Many Indian families have their own recipe for garam masala, and the whole spices are roasted in a wok or on a griddle before grinding. Ready-made garam masala can be bought in large supermarkets and Asian stores.

Ghee

Ghee is clarified butter, and it can be heated to a high temperature without burning. You can buy it easily in Asian stores, and some larger supermarkets. Otherwise use groundnut oil or make it yourself. To make ghee simply put 250g (8 oz) unsalted butter in a saucepan and simmer slowly for about 15 minutes until the butter becomes clear and a whitish residue settles at the bottom. Remove from heat, skim off any scum and allow to cool. Strain off the clear oil (ghee) from the top into a container. Keep in the fridge.

Ginger

Fresh root ginger is used in many Indian dishes. Dried and ground ginger is not a good substitute and shouldn't be used unless the recipe actually calls for it. Fresh ginger needs to be peeled before grating or chopping.

Ginger and Garlic Pastes

These can be bought in jars and conveniently kept in the fridge. The garlic or ginger is very finely chopped and mixed with salt and a little water.

Gram Flour

Sometimes called besan flour, this is a fine yellow flour made from chickpeas. It is used in many Indian dishes such as batters and breads. It is very high in protein and low in gluten.

Mango Powder

Also called amchoor, this consists of raw, sun-dried mango slices that are ground to a powder. It is made from unripe mangos so is quite sour.

Mustard Seeds

These can be bought in three colours; black, brown and yellow.

Yellow mustard seeds can be used in any dish if black or brown are not available, but they tend to be used for lentil and vegetable dishes, especially those containing tomatoes. Black mustard seeds are pungent and used to flavour vegetarian dishes and in yogurt or as a topping. Brown mustard seeds are good in chutneys and toppings.

Rosewater
This is a clear essence extracted from rose petals and it is used to give fragrance to desserts and some rice dishes. It can be bought in chemists, Middle Eastern and Asian stores.

Saffron
The orange coloured stigma of the crocus. An expensive spice which gives a rich yellow colour and exquisite flavour, it is used in rice dishes and desserts. A solution of saffron can be made by crushing the fronds and then steeping them in about 50-85 ml (2-3 fl oz) hot water for 10 minutes. Powdered saffron can also be bought. Turmeric can sometimes be substituted for saffron, but care must be taken not to use too much as it has a stronger and not quite such an exquisite flavour as the saffron.

Tamarind
These are the ripe pods of a large tropical tree. Only the sour tasting pulp inside the pods is needed and the seeds and skin are discarded. The pods are soaked in hot water for 10-15 minutes and then squeezed to extract the pulp.

Lump tamarind can be bought in Indian and Middle Eastern stores and it can be added straight into a dish during cooking or mixed with water first, according to the recipe. It is also possible to buy tamarind paste or concentrate, which can be added directly to recipes. If you cannot find tamarind then lemon juice can be used as a substitute but it does not give quite the same distinctive flavour.

Turmeric
A very important spice in Indian dishes, turmeric is a root which is used occasionally as a vegetable or in pickles but more often is ground and used as a spice. It is bright yellow and should be used with care as too much can give a bitter taste and also it burns easily, especially when 'dry' frying spices before adding the liquid.

White Urad Dhal Flour

This is made from white split gram beans and can be found in Asian stores.

PROBLEM SOLVING

There is very little that can go drastically wrong in Indian recipes, but we all have our 'off' days when things go slightly awry, and so here are some helpful hints on how to 'rescue' your supper!

Lack of colour – some dhal dishes and curries containing dhal can end up looking rather grey and unappealing. The trick is to add a little touch of food colouring, red, yellow or green, depending on the colour of the dhal or main ingredients. If it is a meat curry then try gravy browning or soy sauce. If you don't like the idea of using artificial colourings then try using small amounts of turmeric or paprika to enhance the dish.

Too salty or too hot – it is always best to under salt and add it only at the end or at table, but if you do add too much try adding extra vegetables such as potatoes, peas or tomatoes to soak up the excess. It is a good idea to treat chilli with care until you know how much you like. It is easy to add more, but difficult to tone down too hot a dish. The only answer, if it really is too hot, is to make another batch of the recipe, omitting the chilli, and combine it with the overhot one.

Too sour – add some sweet fruit chutney or a sweet tomato sauce, or even a little white or brown sugar. Add a little at a time, tasting frequently, until a balance has been reached.

Curdling – when yogurt or cream is added to a dish there is always the chance that it may curdle. It is a good idea to mix the yogurt or cream well first so it is smooth. If it is to be added to a hot mixture, draw the dish away from the heat and stir it in slowly. The dish can then be returned to a gentle heat. If the mixture does curdle then strain the contents and allow to cool. Put the ingredients back into the pan. Mix the strained sauce with some more yogurt or cream, add to the pan and heat very gently but do not allow to boil.

Too dry – some 'dry' curries can start to stick to the pan during cooking and you must take care to see that it does not burn. If the food does start to stick, stir in a little boiling water to moisten the mixture.

SERVING AN INDIAN MEAL

A dinner in India is served on a large round silver, brass or stainless steel dish, on which are placed serving bowls containing the curries, rice and dhals etc. Everything is served together and there are ample quantities of rice and bread. It is quite usual for Indians to eat without cutlery, using their right hand only and scooping up food with portions of bread. If you don't wish to eat with your hands, then use plates with a fork and dessert spoon. At the end of a meal serve a dessert and some fresh fruits.

Traditional Indian beverages to go with a meal are Lhassi (yogurt drink), fresh fruit juice, lime juice, or iced water with lemon slices. If you want to serve an alcoholic drink, then try lager, cider, semi-sweet white or rosé wine.

Here is a simple menu outline to use as a guide.

For a special occasion you can increase the number of dishes and have two or three main courses and maybe a choice of desserts.

Aperitif
Poppadums, Crunchy Split Peas

Starter
Onion Bhajias or another starter recipe

Main course
Main dish curry, (meat, chicken, fish or vegetarian) with a dhal dish

Accompaniments
Bread, rice dish, two vegetable dishes, a raitha, one or two chutneys, and a salad

Dessert
Fresh fruit and a dessert

STARTERS AND SNACKS

In India it is usual to eat snacks througout the day. Instead of hamburgers, hot dogs or crisps, Indians will eat samosas, bhajias and kebabs, purchased hot and ready to eat from stalls and kiosks. Many of these dishes make excellent party food as they go so well with drinks, or they can be served as appetisers before a meal. Generally speaking little soup is eaten in India, but there is one that is worth mentioning called Mulligatawny. It comes from the Anglo-Indian community and there are many variations of this hearty soup, which can be eaten on its own with bread as a lunch or supper dish.

COCONUT LAMB KEBABS

REALLY EASY!

Minced lamb well seasoned with cumin, fresh herbs and lemon juice, rolled into balls and grilled until crisp and brown. They make a good appetiser and are very popular with children.

Serves 4

500g (1 lb) lean lamb mince
1 tablespoon tomato purée
3 tablespoons desiccated coconut
1 teaspoon ground cumin
2 tablespoons chopped fresh coriander
1 tablespoon chopped fresh parsley
3 tablespoons lime or lemon juice
freshly ground black pepper

1 Preheat the grill to a medium heat.

2 Place lamb, tomato purée, coconut, cumin, coriander, parsley, lime or lemon juice and black pepper to taste in a large bowl and mix well to combine. Roll mixture into small walnut-sized balls and push onto lightly oiled skewers, leaving gaps between each ball.

3 Cook under the grill for about 15 minutes, turning from time to time, until browned and cooked through.

VEGETABLE SAMOSAS

EASY!

Spicy vegetable filling inside flaky pastry make these a popular snack. Although samosas are traditionally deep-fried, these are more easily cooked in the oven.

Makes 12
2 teaspoons vegetable oil
1 tablespoon curry powder
1 onion, finely chopped
1 tablespoon black mustard seeds
2 teaspoons cumin seeds
2 small potatoes, finely diced
125 ml (4 fl oz) vegetable stock
1 carrot, finely diced
125g (4 oz) fresh or frozen peas
500g (1 lb) prepared puff pastry
1 egg, lightly beaten

1 Heat oil in a large frying pan over a medium heat. Add curry powder, onion, mustard seeds and cumin seeds and cook , stirring, for 3 minutes.

2 Add potatoes and stock to pan and cook, stirring occasionally, for 5 minutes or until potatoes are tender.

3 Add carrot and peas to pan and cook for 2 minutes longer. Remove pan from heat and set aside to cool completely.

4 Preheat oven to 200°C ,400°F,Gas 6. Roll out pastry to 5 mm (¼ inch) thick and, using a 10 cm (4 inch) pastry cutter, cut out 12 rounds. Place spoonfuls of filling on one half of each pastry round, brush edges with egg, fold uncovered half of pastry over filling and press to seal.

5 Place pastries on lightly greased baking trays and bake in the preheated oven for 12-15 minutes or until samosas are puffed and golden.

VEGETABLE BHAJIAS

E A S Y !

**A batter made with eggs, milk, gram (chickpea)
flour, lentils, mixed vegetables and spices, and
then dropped in spoonfuls into hot oil and
cooked until crisp and golden. They are
delicious eaten hot or cold.**

Serves 6
2 eggs, lightly beaten
60 ml (2 fl oz) milk
30g (1 oz) red lentils, washed and cooked
1 red onion, chopped
1 carrot, grated
90g (3 oz) canned sweet corn kernels, drained
1 potato, grated
150g (5 oz) gram (chickpea) flour
¼ teaspoon baking powder
1 teaspoon ground cumin
1 teaspoon ground nutmeg
1 teaspoon ground turmeric
2 tablespoons chopped fresh coriander
vegetable oil for deep-frying

1 Place eggs, milk, lentils, onion, carrot, sweet corn,
potato, flour, baking powder, cumin, nutmeg, turmeric
and coriander in a bowl and mix well to combine.

2 Heat oil in a large saucepan until a cube of bread,
dropped in, browns in 50 seconds. Drop heaped tablespoons of mixture into oil and deep-fry for 2-3 minutes or
until golden. Drain on absorbent kitchen paper.

VEGETABLE SAMOSAS • VEGETABLE BHAJIAS

SPICY INDIAN CHICKEN

REALLY EASY!

Bite-sized pieces of chicken marinated in yogurt with spices and herbs, quickly cooked under a grill and served with a cool, creamy cucumber dip. To make a tasty main dish, simply use whole chicken fillets in this recipe and increase the cooking time.

Serves 8

8 boneless chicken breast fillets, cut into 2.5 cm (1 inch) cubes
170g (6 oz) natural yogurt
1 clove garlic, crushed
1 teaspoon grated fresh ginger
½ teaspoon garam masala
¼ teaspoon ground turmeric
¼ teaspoon ground cumin
1 tablespoon chopped fresh coriander
freshly ground black pepper

Cucumber Coriander Dip

½ cucumber, peeled, grated and drained
1 tablespoon chopped fresh coriander
140g (5 oz) natural yogurt
60 ml (2 fl oz) double cream
freshly ground black pepper

1 Place chicken, yogurt, garlic, ginger, garam masala, turmeric, cumin, coriander and black pepper to taste in a bowl and toss to combine. Cover and refrigerate for at least 4 hours or overnight.

2 Remove chicken from yogurt mixture and place in a single layer on a lightly greased baking tray. Cook under a preheated grill for 5 minutes or until cooked. Spear 1 or 2 pieces of chicken onto wooden toothpicks.

3 To make dip, squeeze excess liquid from cucumber. Place cucumber, coriander, yogurt, cream and black pepper to taste in a bowl and mix to combine. Serve with chicken for dipping.

CRUNCHY SPLIT PEAS

EASY!

Crisp and crunchy deep-fried peas coated in a mixture of salt and spices – ideal as a nibble with drinks. Take care when frying the peas as they tend to make the oil bubble to the top of the pan.

Serves 8

180g (6 oz) yellow split peas (or a mixture of yellow and green split peas)
2 teaspoons bicarbonate of soda
vegetable oil for deep-frying
½ teaspoon chilli powder
½ teaspoon ground coriander
pinch ground cinnamon
pinch ground cloves
1 teaspoon salt

1 Place split peas in a large bowl, cover with water, stir in bicarbonate of soda and set aside to soak overnight.

2 Rinse split peas under cold running water and drain thoroughly. Set aside for at least 30 minutes, then spread out on absorbent kitchen paper to dry. Heat about 5 cm (2 inch) oil in a large frying pan and cook split peas in batches until golden. Using a slotted spoon, remove peas and drain on absorbent kitchen paper.

3 Transfer cooked peas to a dish, sprinkle with chilli powder, coriander, cinnamon, cloves and salt and toss to coat. Allow peas to cool and store in an airtight container.

ONION BHAJIAS

EASY!

A thick gram (chickpea) flour batter, flavoured with finely chopped onions and dropped in spoonfuls into hot oil and cooked until crisp and golden.

Serves 6
125g (4 oz) gram (chickpea) flour
2 medium onions, finely chopped
1 teaspoon chopped fresh coriander
½ teaspoon ground turmeric
½ teaspoon paprika
¼ teaspoon bicarbonate of soda
¼ teaspoon salt
about 150 ml (¼ pint) water
vegetable oil for deep-frying

1 Put flour, onions, coriander, turmeric, paprika, bicarbonate of soda and salt into a bowl. Mix together. Gradually mix in enough water to make a thick batter. Leave to stand for 5 minutes.

2 Heat oil in a large saucepan until a cube of bread, dropped in, browns in 50 seconds. Drop heaped tablespoons of mixture into oil and deep-fry for about 2-3 minutes until golden brown and crisp.

POPPADUMS

EASY!

**Thin flat wafers that are deep-fried until crisp
and golden. They are good to serve with meals,
but are also especially enjoyable with chutney or
raitha as an appetiser. They can be bought either
partially or fully prepared.**

*1 packet partially prepared Poppadums
vegetable oil for deep-frying*

1 Heat the oil in a deep saucepan or wok. Carefully drop in one poppadum at a time. The oil should sizzle and the poppadum should expand at once, if not, the oil is not hot enough. Cook for a few seconds until crisp and golden brown. Remove and drain on kitchen paper and continue cooking the remaining poppadums. Serve at once while still crisp.

VEGETABLE PAKORIS

EASY!

Small pieces of vegetable coated in batter and deep-fried until crisp, these fritters are similar to Japanese tempura. They can be made in advance and reheated by briefly refrying for 1-2 minutes or by heating in a moderate oven.

Serves 6-8

150g (5 oz) gram (chickpea) flour
½ teaspoon bicarbonate of soda
½ teaspoon ground turmeric
½ teaspoon paprika
½ teaspoon ground coriander
¼ teaspoon salt
about 250 ml (8 fl oz) water
vegetable oil for frying
about 1 kg (2 lb) assorted vegetables such as potato, cauliflower, aubergine, red or green peppers, carrot, courgette etc, cut into large bite-size pieces

1 Put the gram (chickpea) flour, bicarbonate of soda, turmeric, paprika, coriander and salt into a bowl and mix well together. Gradually add enough water to mix to a smooth coating batter.

2 Heat the oil in a large saucepan until a cube of bread, dropped in, browns in 50 seconds. Pat the vegetables dry with kitchen paper and then dip a few in the batter. Fry them a few at a time in the hot oil for about 5 minutes until cooked through and golden brown.

MULLIGATAWNY SOUP

EASY!

**A thick soup made with vegetables and lamb
that has a spicy, fruity flavour given by the
addition of curry powder, apple and lemon juice.
Hearty enough to be a meal in its own right, it
can be thinned down with a little extra stock or
milk and served as a starter.**

Serves 4-6

30g (1 oz) ghee or butter
2 onions, finely chopped
2 carrots, finely chopped
250g (8 oz) lean lamb or chicken mince
2 large tomatoes, skinned and chopped
1 small cooking apple, peeled, cored and chopped
1-2 tablespoons curry powder
1 litre (1¾ pints) beef or chicken stock
salt
freshly ground black pepper
2 tablespoons gram (chickpea) flour
150 ml (¼ pint) milk or coconut milk
30g (1 oz) cooked rice
1-2 tablespoons lemon juice

1 Heat ghee or butter in a large saucepan and cook the
onions gently for about 5 minutes until soft. Add the
carrots and lamb (or chicken) and cook for 2-3 minutes,
stirring, until lamb has turned brown. Stir in tomatoes,
apple and curry powder and cook for a minute. Gradually
stir in stock and seasoning to taste. Cover and simmer
gently for 30 minutes.

2 Remove from heat and cool slightly. Put into a food
processor or blender and process until smooth. Return
to pan. Blend gram (chickpea) flour and milk together
and stir into the soup. Bring to the boil, stirring. Cook

gently for 5 minutes. Stir in cooked rice and lemon juice, and adjust seasoning if necessary, and serve.

MEAT CURRIES

The most popular meat in India is lamb, as both beef and pork are forbidden by certain religions and so are not eaten quite as much. Meat is often marinated in yogurt and spices to tenderise it and allow the flavours of the spices to penetrate. The addition of yogurt also helps to thicken the sauce. Always use lean meat for curries, trimming off any fat. Many of the recipes are cooked with very little liquid other than that which comes naturally from the marinade or meat juices. These curries should be watched whilst cooking to make sure they do not burn, and a little water can be added if they appear too dry.

LAMB IN SPINACH SAUCE

EASY!

Finely chopped lamb cooked with puréed tomatoes, garlic, chilli and spices, with finely chopped fresh spinach added in the final stage of cooking.

Serves 4

6 large ripe tomatoes, skinned and roughly chopped
2 tablespoons vegetable oil
2 teaspoons finely chopped fresh ginger
3 fresh red or green chillies, finely chopped
3 cloves garlic, finely chopped
salt
500g (1 lb) lean lamb, finely chopped
¼ teaspoon ground cumin
¼ teaspoon ground coriander
¼ teaspoon ground cinnamon
¼ teaspoon ground cloves
¼ teaspoon mango powder
¼ teaspoon ground turmeric
1 kg (2 lb) fresh spinach, finely chopped

1 Place tomatoes in a food processor or blender and process until smooth.

2 Heat oil in a heavy-based saucepan, add ginger, chillies, garlic and salt to taste and cook, stirring, for 2 minutes. Add lamb and mix well. Cover and cook over a low heat for 30-40 minutes or until lamb is tender.

3 Stir in tomatoes and cook for 10 minutes. Add cumin, coriander, cinnamon, cloves, mango powder and turmeric and cook over a low heat, stirring occasionally, for 10 minutes. Add spinach and cook for 5 minutes longer.

LAMB KEBABS

E A S Y !

Cubes of lamb marinated with lemon juice, garlic and spices, threaded on to skewers and grilled, and served with a hot and spicy Tomato and Onion Sauce.

Serves 6

1 kg (2 lb) lean lamb, cut into 2.5 cm (1 inch) cubes
salt
2 tablespoons lemon juice
2 cloves garlic, finely chopped
2 teaspoons finely chopped fresh ginger
2 fresh red chillies, finely chopped
1 teaspoon garam masala
1 teaspoon ground cumin
1 teaspoon ground coriander
1 teaspoon mango powder
½ teaspoon ground turmeric

Tomato And Onion Sauce

3 large onions, roughly chopped
1 tablespoon vegetable oil
2 cloves garlic, finely chopped
2 teaspoons finely chopped fresh ginger
2 fresh red or green chillies, finely chopped
3 large tomatoes, chopped
1 teaspoon garam masala
1 teaspoon ground cumin
1 teaspoon ground coriander
1 teaspoon mango powder
½ teaspoon ground turmeric
2 teaspoons cumin seeds
2-3 tablespoons chopped fresh coriander

1 Place lamb, salt to taste, lemon juice, garlic, ginger, chillies, garam masala, cumin, ground coriander, mango powder and turmeric in a bowl, mix to combine, cover and set aside to marinate for 2-3 hours.

2 To make sauce, place onions in a food processor or blender and process to form a purée. Heat oil in a heavy-based saucepan, add garlic, ginger and chillies and cook over a low heat, stirring, for 1 minute. Stir in onion purée and cook for 7-10 minutes or until onions are soft and slightly browned. Add tomatoes and cook for 10 minutes or until tomatoes are soft and pulpy. Stir in garam masala, ground cumin, ground coriander, mango powder, turmeric, cumin seeds and fresh coriander and cook for 5 minutes longer.

3 Thread lamb onto 12 lightly oiled skewers and cook under a preheated medium grill, turning frequently, for 5-7 minutes or until just cooked. To serve, place kebabs on a serving dish and either pour over the sauce or serve it separately.

MOGUL LAMB

EASY!

A whole leg of lamb marinated in a spicy tomato sauce and then cooked in the same sauce until tender.

Serves 6

15g (½ oz) butter
750g (1½ lb) ripe tomatoes, skinned and finely chopped
2-3 fresh red or green chillies, finely chopped
2 teaspoons finely chopped fresh ginger
4 cloves garlic, finely chopped
salt
1 teaspoon freshly ground black pepper
½ teaspoon ground cardamom
½ teaspoon ground cloves
½ teaspoon ground fennel
½ teaspoon ground cinnamon
½ teaspoon ground fenugreek
125 ml (4 fl oz) water
4 tablespoons chopped fresh coriander
1 tablespoon chopped fresh basil
2 tablespoons chopped fresh mint
1 teaspoon chopped fresh dill
1 x 1.5 kg (3 lb) leg lamb

1 Melt butter in a large saucepan, add tomatoes, chillies, ginger, garlic and salt to taste and cook over a medium heat, stirring frequently, for 15 minutes or until tomatoes are soft and pulpy.

2 Place black pepper, cardamom, cloves, fennel, cinnamon, fenugreek and water in a bowl and mix well to combine. Stir spice mixture into tomato mixture, then add coriander, basil, mint and dill. Remove sauce from heat and set aside to become cold. Place lamb in a glass or ceramic baking dish, pour over sauce, cover and marinate in the refrigerator for 15-20 hours.

3 Preheat the oven to 180C, 350F, Gas 4. Remove cover from baking dish and bake lamb in the preheated oven for 2 hours or until tender.

LAMB KORMA

E A S Y !

A mild creamy dish of lamb marinated in yogurt, garlic and turmeric and then cooked gently with spices, coconut and very little liquid. Kormas are spicy rather than hot and can be made with chicken or beef as well as lamb.

Serves 4

170g (6 oz) natural yogurt
2 cloves garlic, finely chopped
2 teaspoons turmeric
500g (1 lb) lean lamb, cut into cubes
60g (2 oz) ghee or butter
1 onion, chopped
2 teaspoons chopped fresh ginger
1 cinnamon stick
8-10 cloves
5 whole cardamoms, split
1 teaspoon ground coriander
1 teaspoon ground cumin
½ teaspoon chilli powder
1 tablespoon desiccated coconut
salt
about 150 ml (¼ pint) water

1 Put yogurt, garlic, and turmeric into a bowl and mix well together. Add the lamb and stir well. Cover and leave in a cool place to marinate overnight.

2 Melt the ghee in a pan and add the onion and cook for about 5 minutes until soft. Stir in the ginger, cinnamon stick, cloves, cardamoms, coriander, cumin, and chilli. Cook for 2-3 minutes.

3 Add the lamb and marinade to the pan, together with the coconut and salt to taste. Add the water and bring to the boil. Cover with a tight-fitting lid and simmer gently for about 40 minutes until lamb is tender. Add a little more water during cooking if the lamb is too dry.

BALTI LAMB

EASY!

Lamb and onions are stir-fried in a balti pan or wok, together with whole and ground spices and vegetables. A spicy tomato sauce is stirred in and the mixture is cooked gently and served piping hot in the balti pan.

Serves 4

Balti Sauce
2 tablespoons vegetable oil
1 onion, chopped
2 cloves garlic, finely chopped
1 tablespoon finely chopped fresh ginger
2 green chillies, chopped
6 whole cloves
2 cardamoms, crushed
2 teaspoons ground coriander
1 teaspoon paprika
1 teaspoon ground cinnamon
1 teaspoon ground turmeric
½ teaspoon ground cumin
225g (8 oz) can chopped tomatoes and their juice
300 ml (½ pint) vegetable stock
1 tablespoon lemon juice

2 tablespoons vegetable oil
1 onion, chopped
500g (1 lb) lean lamb, cubed
1 tablespoon dried crushed chillies
½ teaspoon ground nutmeg
1 teaspoon fennel seeds
1 teaspoon black onion seeds
1 red pepper, seeded and cut into 2.5 cm
(1 inch) squares

*2 medium potatoes, cut into 2.5 cm (1 inch) cubes,
par-boiled and then fried in a little oil until golden
2 tablespoons chopped fresh coriander*

1 To make the sauce, heat 2 tablespoons oil in a pan and cook the onion, garlic and ginger for about 5 minutes. Add the chillies and cook for 2 minutes. Add cloves, cardamom, coriander, paprika, cinnamon, turmeric and cumin. Cook for a minute. Stir in tomatoes, stock and lemon juice. Bring to the boil. Simmer gently, uncovered, for 30 minutes. Remove from heat and set aside.

2 Heat 2 tablespoons oil over a high heat in a balti pan or wok. Fry the onion for 2-3 minutes. Add the lamb and cook for 5 minutes. Add the dried chillies, nutmeg,fennel seeds, black onion seeds and red pepper and cook 2-3 minutes. Pour in the balti sauce and cook gently for about 15 minutes until lamb is tender. Stir in the potatoes and fresh coriander and heat for 3-4 minutes. Serve in the balti pan.

LAMB ROGAN JOSH

Small cubes of lamb marinated in yogurt and then cooked with a spiced almond paste, curry spices and tomatoes. A rich well-flavoured dish.

Serves 4
500g (1 lb) lean lamb, cut into 2.5 cm (1 inch) cubes
170g (6 oz) natural yogurt

Spice Paste
1 tablespoon chopped fresh ginger
4 cloves garlic
¼ teaspoon ground nutmeg
large pinch ground cloves
10 black peppercorns
60g (2 oz) blanched almonds
2 cardamom pods

2 tablespoons vegetable oil
1 onion, chopped
½ teaspoon ground turmeric
½ teaspoon chilli powder
1 teaspoon ground cumin
1 teaspoon paprika
1 teaspoon ground coriander
salt
225g (8 oz) can chopped tomatoes and their juice

1 Put lamb in a bowl, add yogurt and mix well. Cover and leave in a cool place overnight.

2 Using a pestle and mortar or a food processor, grind together the ginger, garlic, nutmeg, cloves, peppercorns, almonds and cardamoms, adding a little water to make a paste.

3 Heat oil in a pan and fry onion for about 5 minutes until soft. Stir in Spice Paste and cook gently for a minute. Add turmeric, chilli powder, cumin, paprika, coriander and salt and cook for a minute. Add lamb and marinade and the tomatoes. Stir well.

4 Cover tightly and simmer gently for 40-50 minutes until the meat is tender and the sauce is fairly thick. If the mixture becomes too dry during cooking, add a little water.

LAMB ROGAN JOSH

LAMB PASANDA

EASY!

Lamb marinated in yogurt and spices and then cooked gently until tender. Cashew nut paste and double cream is stirred in at the end of the cooking time, and the dish sprinkled with lemon juice and sliced chilli.

Serves 4

500g (1 lb) lean lamb, cut into thin 2.5 cm
(1 inch) strips
140g (5 oz) natural yogurt
3-4 cloves garlic, finely chopped
1 tablespoon chopped fresh ginger
1 teaspoon ground coriander
2 teaspoons ground cumin
1 teaspoon garam masala
salt
2 tablespoons vegetable oil
1 onion, chopped
1 teaspoon chilli powder
150 ml (¼ pint) water
4 tablespoons cashew nuts, ground to a paste with a little milk in a pestle and mortar
125 ml (4 fl oz) double cream
lemon juice
2 fresh green chillies, de-seeded and finely sliced

1 Put lamb, yogurt, garlic, ginger, coriander, cumin, garam masala and a little salt into a bowl and mix together. Cover and leave to marinate for 1-2 hours.

2 Heat oil in a pan and fry the onion for 5 minutes until soft. Stir in the chilli powder and cook for a minute. Stir in the meat and marinade and cook until meat begins to brown. Stir in the water. Cover and simmer gently for 40-45 minutes until meat is tender.

3 Just before serving, stir in the cashew paste and double cream and heat gently without boiling. Sprinkle over a little lemon juice and scatter the sliced chillies over the top.

LAMB PULLAO

Lamb fillets sealed and then marinated in yogurt
with onions and spices. After baking until tender
in the marinade, the lamb is served on a large
platter with mounds of coloured and flavoured
rice, and garnished with fried cumin seeds,
almonds, cashews, pistachios, sultanas,
egg slices, coriander and lemon. This is a very
special dish usually served for festive occasions
and banquets, so you do need time for
all the preparation.

Serves 6-8
3 tablespoons vegetable oil
salt
1 kg (2 lb) lamb fillets
1 litre (1¾ pint) water
2 onions, thinly sliced
2 teaspoons chopped fresh ginger
5 cloves garlic, chopped
2 fresh green chillies, finely chopped
½ teaspoon ground cumin
½ teaspoon ground cardamom
½ teaspoon ground nutmeg
½ teaspoon ground cloves
pinch turmeric
500g (1 lb) natural yogurt

Spice Bags
8 cloves
2 sticks cinnamon
12 green cardamom pods or 2 large black
cardamom pods
6 dried red chillies
4 bay leaves

½ teaspoon coriander seeds
½ teaspoon cumin seeds
½ teaspoon black peppercorns
2 pieces muslin, each 12-15 cm (5-6 inch) square

Rice
400 g (14 oz) long-grain rice
pinch tandoori colouring or red food colouring
pinch turmeric
2 drops green food colouring

Garnish
1 tablespoon vegetable oil
1½ teaspoons black cumin seeds
30g (1 oz) fried blanched almond slivers
30g (1 oz) fried or salted cashews
150g (5 oz) chopped pistachios
60g (2 oz) fried sultanas
2 onions, sliced and fried
3 hard-boiled eggs, thinly sliced
2 tablespoons chopped fresh coriander
1 lemon, cut into wedges (optional)

1 To make Spice Bags, place half the cloves, cinnamon sticks, cardamom pods, chillies, bay leaves, coriander seeds, cumin seeds and black peppercorns on each piece of muslin. Draw up corners and tie securely. Set aside.

2 Heat 1 tablespoon oil, salt to taste and 1 spice bag in a large deep saucepan. Add lamb fillets and water and bring to the boil over a high heat. Remove meat and spice bag. Pat meat dry and set aside. Strain cooking liquid and reserve for cooking rice.

3 Heat remaining oil in a large frying pan, add onions, ginger, garlic and chillies and cook over a medium heat, stirring, for 10 minutes or until onions are soft. Stir in cumin, cardamom, nutmeg, cloves and turmeric. Transfer onion mixture to a bowl, stir in yogurt and 2 tablespoons water and set aside.

4 Heat the same frying pan over a high heat, add lamb fillets and cook quickly on all sides to seal. Remove fillets and place in a baking dish. Spoon yogurt mixture over fillets, cover and refrigerate for 4 hours.

5 Preheat the oven to 180C,350F,Gas 4. Remove cover from baking dish and bake for 30-35 minutes or until lamb is tender.

6 To cook rice, place rice in an ovenproof dish. Measure reserved cooking liquid and add enough water to make up to 1.2 litres (2 pints) liquid. Add to rice with remaining spice bag and salt to taste and bake at 160C,325F,Gas 3 for 45 minutes or until rice is cooked. Divide rice into four portions. Mix tandoori colouring with a little water and mix into one portion of rice to make red-coloured rice. Mix turmeric with a little water and mix into a second portion of rice to make yellow-coloured rice. Mix green food colouring with a little water and mix into third portion of rice to make green rice. Leave remaining portion of rice plain.

7 To serve, place lamb with juices in centre of a large flat platter. Surround with mounds of rice. For the garnish, heat 1 tablespoon oil in a soup ladle or very small pan, and pour in black cumin seeds. Allow to sizzle then remove from heat and pour over rice. Sprinkle with almonds, cashews, pistachios, sultanas and onions. Cover lamb with egg slices and sprinkle with fresh coriander. Surround with lemon wedges (if using) and serve.

CARDAMOM LAMB

REALLY EASY!

Lean diced lamb, carrots and onions with spices, chilli paste and coconut milk.

Serves 4

2 tablespoons vegetable oil
3 carrots, sliced
3 onions, sliced
750g (1½ lb) lean diced lamb
1 tablespoon flour
1 bay leaf, crumbled
1 teaspoon ground cardamom
2 teaspoons ground cumin
1 teaspoon chilli paste (sambal oelek)
250 ml (8 fl oz) coconut milk
freshly ground black pepper

1 Preheat the oven to 150C,300F,Gas 2. Heat oil in a large frying pan and cook carrots and onions over a medium heat for 5 minutes or until onions are soft. Transfer to a large casserole dish.

2 Toss lamb in flour and shake off excess. Add meat to pan and cook over a high heat for 5 minutes or until browned on all sides. Transfer meat to casserole dish.

3 Add bay leaf, cardamom, cumin, chilli paste (sambal oelek) and coconut milk to casserole and mix to combine. Bake in the preheated oven for 1½-2 hours or until meat is tender. Season to taste with black pepper.

MEAT KEBABS WITH YOGURT

EASY!

Minced meat rissoles made with spices, cream and egg, cooked and and then served with a yogurt sauce and dry spice topping.

Serves 4-6

Meat Kebabs
750g (1½ lb) lamb, beef or chicken mince
¼ teaspoon ground cloves
¼ teaspoon ground cinnamon
¼ teaspoon ground cardamom
¼ teaspoon ground nutmeg
½ teaspoon ground cumin
½ teaspoon ground coriander
½ teaspoon mango powder
½ teaspoon paprika
½ teaspoon ground ginger
salt
125 ml (4 fl oz) double cream
1 egg, size 3
2 tablespoons chopped fresh coriander
vegetable oil for deep-frying
170g (6 oz) natural yogurt
60 ml (2 fl oz) water

Dry Spice Garnish
¼ teaspoon mango powder
¼ teaspoon paprika
¼ teaspoon caster sugar
¼ teaspoon black salt
salt
1 tablespoon chopped fresh coriander

1 To make kebabs, place mince, cloves, cinnamon,

cardamom, nutmeg, cumin, ground coriander, mango powder, paprika, ginger and salt to taste in a bowl and knead well. Add cream, 1 tablespoon at a time, kneading well after each addition. Break egg into mince mixture and knead for a few minutes longer. Set aside to stand for 15 minutes. Add fresh coriander to mince mixture and knead well. Take small portions of mince mixture and, using wet hands, form into oval-shaped kebabs about 5 cm (2 inch) long.

2 Place kebabs in a steamer set over a wok or saucepan of simmering water and steam for 15-25 minutes or until cooked. Remove kebabs from steamer and set aside.

3 Heat 2.5 cm (1 inch) oil in a heavy-based frying pan and cook kebabs quickly until golden. Transfer kebabs to a serving dish, set aside and keep warm.

4 Place yogurt and water in a bowl and beat until smooth. Spoon yogurt mixture over kebabs.

5 For garnish, combine mango powder, paprika, sugar, black salt and salt to taste. Sprinkle spice mixture and fresh coriander over kebabs.

MEAT KEBABS WITH YOGURT

MINTED TANDOORI CUTLETS

REALLY EASY!

**Lamb chump chops, cut into three and marinated
in spiced yogurt then baked in the oven and
served sprinkled with chopped fresh mint.**

Serves 4

*8 lamb chump chops, each cut into 3 pieces
2 tablespoons chopped fresh mint*

Tandoori Marinade

*170g (6 oz) natural yogurt
1 tablespoon ground cumin
1 tablespoon ground coriander
2 tablespoons curry powder
freshly ground black pepper*

1 To make marinade, place yogurt, cumin, coriander,
curry powder and black pepper to taste in a bowl and
mix to combine. Add lamb pieces and toss to coat. Cover
and set aside to marinate for 1-2 hours or overnight in
the refrigerator.

2 Preheat oven to 180C,350F,Gas 4.

3 Place lamb pieces on a rack set in a baking dish and
bake in the preheated oven, turning every 15 minutes,
for about 40 minutes or until lamb is tender. Sprinkle
lamb with mint and serve immediately.

PORK VINDALOO

EASY!

**Pork dishes are few and far between in India,
but this is a well-known dish that is very hot and
spicy and should be served with yogurt
or a raitha.**

Serves 6

1 kg (2 lb) lean pork, diced
2 onions, chopped
3 cloves garlic, crushed
400g (14 oz) canned tomatoes, undrained and chopped
2 teaspoons ground cumin
2 teaspoons mustard seeds
2 teaspoons ground cinnamon
1 teaspoon ground turmeric
1-2 teaspoons chilli paste (sambal oelek)
60 ml (2 fl oz) white vinegar
1 tablespoon brown sugar
3 tablespoons natural yogurt
2 tablespoons lime juice
freshly ground black pepper
500 ml (16 fl oz) chicken stock
2 tablespoons chopped fresh coriander

1 Place pork, onions, garlic, tomatoes, cumin, mustard seeds, cinnamon, turmeric, chilli paste (sambal oelek), vinegar, sugar, yogurt, lime juice and black pepper to taste in a glass or ceramic bowl and mix to combine. Cover and marinate in the refrigerator for at least 3 hours.

2 Transfer pork mixture to a large saucepan, stir in stock and bring to simmering. Cover and simmer, stirring occasionally, for 1 hour or until pork is tender. Just prior to serving, stir in coriander.

DRY BEEF CURRY

EASY!

A hot spicy beef curry that is cooked with only a little water so it is 'dry' in consistency. This is a traditional type of curry and any cubed meat such as lamb, pork or chicken can be used, adjusting the cooking time as necessary.

Serves 4
60g (2 oz) ghee or butter
500g (1 lb) braising steak, cubed
1 large onion, chopped
2 fresh red chillies, sliced
2 cloves garlic, crushed
1 teaspoon ground coriander
1 teaspoon saffron powder
1 teaspoon ground cumin
1 teaspoon black mustard seeds
1 tablespoon garam masala
125 ml (4 fl oz) water
2 large tomatoes, skinned and chopped
2 curry leaves (optional)
1 small cinnamon stick
3 tablespoons natural yogurt

1 To make curry, melt 45g (1½ oz) ghee or butter in a large saucepan and cook meat in batches until brown on all sides. Remove meat from pan and set aside.

2 Melt remaining ghee or butter in pan, add onion and chillies and cook for 4-5 minutes or until onion is golden. Stir in garlic, coriander, saffron, cumin, mustard seeds and half the garam masala and cook for 1 minute longer.

3 Stir water, tomatoes, curry leaves and cinnamon stick into pan and bring to the boil. Reduce heat to simmering, return meat to pan, cover and simmer for 1½ hours or until meat is tender.

4 Remove pan from heat, stir in remaining garam masala and yogurt. Return pan to heat and simmer for 5 minutes. Remove cinnamon stick and curry leaves, if used, before serving.

EASY BEEF AND TOMATO CURRY

REALLY EASY!

A simple curried beef made with curry powder, spices, tomato purée, chutney and tomatoes.

Serves 4-6

3 tablespoons vegetable oil
750g (1½ lb) braising steak, cut into wide strips
3 onions, chopped
3 cloves garlic, crushed
1 tablespoon curry powder
1 tablespoon cumin seeds
2 teaspoons ground coriander
2 tablespoons tomato purée
1 tablespoon sweet fruit chutney
400g (14 oz) canned tomatoes, undrained and mashed
250 ml (8 fl oz) beef stock

1 Heat oil in a large frying pan, add meat and cook over a high heat for 4-5 minutes or until meat is browned. Remove meat from pan and set aside.

2 Reduce heat to medium, add onions and garlic to pan and cook, stirring, for 4-5 minutes or until onions are soft. Add curry powder and cook for 1 minute longer. Return beef to the pan, then add cumin seeds, coriander, tomato purée, chutney, tomatoes and stock and bring to the boil. Reduce heat, cover and simmer, stirring occasionally, for 1 hour or until meat is tender.

BEEF MADRAS

EASY!

Cubes of beef coated and cooked in a hot chilli paste and then simmered gently with coconut milk and stock.

Serves 6
1 tablespoon vegetable oil
1.5 kg (3 lb) topside or top rump steak, trimmed of all visible fat, cut into 3 cm (1¼ inch) cubes
300 ml (10 fl oz) coconut milk
500 ml (16 fl oz) beef stock

Chilli Paste
1 tablespoon coriander seeds
1 tablespoon cumin seeds
2 fresh red chillies, de-seeded and chopped
12 fresh curry leaves or 6 dried curry leaves
2 cloves garlic
1 tablespoon fresh lime juice
1 tablespoon brown sugar
3 tablespoons water

1 To make paste, place coriander seeds, cumin seeds, chillies, curry leaves, garlic, lime juice, sugar and water in a food processor or blender and process to make a smooth paste. Alternatively, use a pestle and mortar to make the paste.

2 Heat oil in a large saucepan over a high heat. Add paste and cook, stirring, for 1 minute. Add steak, stir to coat evenly with paste and cook, stirring, for 4 minutes.

3 Add coconut milk and stock to pan and bring to simmering over a medium heat. Simmer, stirring occasionally, for 1 hour or until steak is tender. Add extra stock if curry becomes too dry during cooking.

BEEF KOFTA

E A S Y !

Spicy meat rissoles made with beef, cooked in a creamy sauce with chillies, garlic, curry spices and fresh coriander.

Serves 6
1 kg (2 lb) beef mince
2 tablespoons double cream
2 teaspoons finely chopped fresh ginger
2 fresh red or green chillies, finely chopped
3 cloves garlic, finely chopped
1 teaspoon mango powder
1½ teaspoons ground coriander
1½ teaspoons garam masala
1¼ teaspoons ground cumin
salt

Cream Sauce
1 tablespoon vegetable oil
1 teaspoon cumin seeds
2 bay leaves
2 teaspoons finely chopped fresh ginger
2 fresh red or green chillies, finely chopped
3 cloves garlic, finely chopped
284 ml (10 fl oz) double cream
1 teaspoon mango powder
½ teaspoon ground turmeric
1¼ teaspoons ground coriander
½ teaspoon garam masala
1¼ teaspoons ground cumin
2-3 tablespoons chopped fresh coriander
salt

1 To make kofta, place mince, cream, ginger, chillies, garlic, mango powder, ground coriander, garam masala, cumin and salt to taste in a bowl and mix well to combine. Take spoonfuls of mixture and, using wet hands, mould mixture into oval shapes or rissoles and place in a steamer. Three-quarters fill a saucepan with water and bring to the boil. Place steamer over saucepan, cover and steam for 15-20 minutes or until kofta is just cooked.

2 Remove kofta from steamer and place in a shallow ovenproof dish. Set aside. Preheat oven to 150C, 300F, Gas 2.

3 To make sauce, heat oil in a saucepan over a low heat, add cumin seeds, bay leaves, ginger, chillies and garlic and cook for 2 minutes. Stir in cream, mango powder, turmeric, ground coriander, garam masala and cumin and cook, stirring constantly, for 5-7 minutes. Remove sauce from heat, stir in fresh coriander and season to taste with salt. Spoon sauce over kofta, cover and bake in the preheated oven for 20 minutes.

CHICKEN CURRIES

In most Indian recipes, chicken is skinned and
cut into small portions or chunks so that the
spices can penetrate and thoroughly coat the
pieces. Chicken takes well to being marinated
and then cooked quickly as in a tikka dish or
tandoori style, and is equally good in a curry or
with rice in a biryani.

TANDOORI CHICKEN

REALLY EASY!

**Chicken pieces marinated in yogurt and spices
and then baked in the oven.**

Serves 4
12 chicken thigh fillets, skinned

Tandoori Paste
*170g (6 oz) natural yogurt
1 tablespoon paprika
3 teaspoons garam masala
1 teaspoon chilli powder
1 tablespoon grated fresh ginger
2 cloves garlic, crushed
2 teaspoons ground cumin*

1 To make paste, place yogurt, paprika, garam masala, chilli powder, ginger, garlic and cumin in a bowl and mix to combine.

2 Place chicken in a large shallow glass or ceramic dish. Spoon paste over chicken. Turn to coat with marinade, cover and refrigerate for at least 2 hours.

3 Preheat oven to 200°C, 400°F, Gas 6. Remove chicken from dish, leaving on the coating of marinade, and place on a wire rack set in a baking dish. Pour enough water into baking dish to one-third fill it and bake in the preheated oven for 30 minutes or until chicken is cooked and tender.

CHICKEN BIRYANI

EASY!

The Muslim emperors of India between 1526 and 1857 were called the Great Moguls, and at lavish feasts they would serve enormous plates of biryanis. It is a substantial meal of rice, spiced chicken, yogurt, cream and cashew nuts.

Serves 4

90g (3 oz) ghee or butter
3 onions, sliced
1.5 kg (3 lb) chicken pieces
2 teaspoons grated fresh ginger
3 cloves garlic, crushed
½ teaspoon ground cumin
½ teaspoon ground cinnamon
¼ teaspoon ground cloves
¼ teaspoon ground cardamom
¼ teaspoon ground nutmeg
½ teaspoon flour
250 ml (8 fl oz) chicken stock
125g (4 oz) natural yogurt
125 ml (4 fl oz) double cream
60g (2 oz) roasted cashew nuts, chopped

Rice Pilau

60g (2 oz) ghee or butter
½ teaspoon ground saffron
½ teaspoon ground cardamom
1 teaspoon salt
200g (7 oz) basmati rice, well washed
l litre (1¾ pints) chicken stock
2 tablespoons sultanas

1 Heat ghee or butter in a large frying pan and cook onions, stirring, over a medium heat for 5 minutes or until golden. Remove from pan and set aside. Add chicken to pan and cook for 3-4 minutes each side or until golden. Remove from pan and set aside.

2 Add ginger, garlic, cumin, cinnamon, cloves, cardamom, nutmeg and flour to pan and cook, stirring, for 1-2 minutes. Add stock, yogurt and cream, stirring to lift sediment from base of pan. Return chicken and half the onion mixture to pan, cover and simmer for 15-20 minutes or until chicken is just cooked. Remove pan from heat and stand, covered, for 15 minutes.

3 Preheat the oven to 180C,350F,Gas 4. To make pilau, melt ghee or butter in a large saucepan and cook saffron, cardamom, salt and rice, stirring constantly, for 1-2 minutes. Add stock and bring to the boil. Stir in sultanas, reduce heat and simmer for 10-15 minutes or until most of the stock is absorbed and rice is cooked. Cover and set aside to stand for 10 minutes.

4 Place rice on a large ovenproof serving platter, top with chicken pieces and spoon sauce over. Sprinkle with remaining onions and cashew nuts, cover and bake in the preheated oven for 20 minutes.

HOT CHICKEN AND POTATO CURRY

EASY!

**New potatoes cooked with chicken in a
tomato curry sauce.**

Serves 4

10 new potatoes, peeled and halved
2 onions, cut into eighths
1 clove garlic, crushed
½ teaspoon curry paste (vindaloo)
400g (14 oz) canned tomatoes, undrained and mashed
250 ml (8 fl oz) chicken stock
2 tablespoons dry white wine
2 tablespoons mango chutney
3 teaspoons curry powder
2 teaspoons ground cumin
4 tablespoons tomato purée
2 chicken breast fillets, cut into 2.5 cm (1 inch) cubes
1 tablespoon finely chopped fresh coriander

1 Boil or steam potatoes until just tender. Set aside to cool.

2 Place onions, garlic, curry paste and 1 tablespoon of juice from tomatoes in a saucepan and cook for 2-3 minutes, or until onion is soft.

3 Combine tomatoes, stock, wine, chutney, curry powder, cumin and tomato purée. Stir into onion mixture and cook over a medium heat for 2-3 minutes. Add chicken and potatoes and cook over a low heat for about 15 minutes, or until chicken is tender. Just prior to serving sprinkle with coriander.

CHICKEN COCONUT CURRY

EASY!

Cubes of chicken breast cooked in a curried, coconut milk sauce with chillies.

Serves 6
1 tablespoon vegetable oil
2 teaspoons cumin seeds
2 teaspoons finely chopped fresh ginger
2-3 fresh red or green chillies, finely chopped
4-5 cloves garlic, finely chopped
500g (1 lb) boneless skinned chicken breast fillets, cubed
1 teaspoon ground turmeric
1 teaspoon mango powder
1 teaspoon ground cumin
1 teaspoon ground coriander
½ teaspoon garam masala
pinch ground cloves
pinch ground cinnamon
pinch ground cardamom
400 ml (14 fl oz) coconut milk
salt

1 Heat oil in a heavy-based saucepan over a low heat, add cumin seeds, ginger, chillies and garlic and cook, stirring, for 1 minute.

2 Add chicken, mix well, cover and cook, stirring occasionally, for 20 minutes or until chicken is tender.

3 Stir in turmeric mango powder, ground cumin, coriander, garam masala, cloves, cinnamon and cardamom and cook, stirring, for 3-5 minutes. Add coconut milk, bring to simmering and season to taste with salt. Remove pan from heat and serve.

CHICKEN MADRAS

EASY!

**Chicken pieces marinated in lime juice and chilli,
then cooked in a hot spicy sauce.**

Serves 4

1.5 kg (3 lb) chicken, cut into 8 and skinned

Marinade

2 tablespoons fresh lime juice
1 teaspoon chilli powder
freshly ground black pepper

30g (1 oz) ghee or butter
1 tablespoon vegetable oil
1 large onion, finely chopped
2 cloves garlic, finely chopped
2 teaspoons chopped fresh ginger
2 teaspoons ground coriander
2 teaspoons ground cumin
1 teaspoon ground turmeric
1 teaspoon chilli powder
salt
150 ml (¼ pint) water
2 teaspoons garam masala

1 Put chicken into a large bowl. Mix together the lime juice, chilli powder and pepper and pour over chicken. Mix well, cover and leave in a cool place for 3-4 hours.

2 Heat the ghee and oil in a large pan and cook the onion, garlic and ginger gently for about 5 minutes until soft. Add the coriander, cumin, turmeric and chilli and cook for a minute.

3 Add the chicken and marinade and brown the pieces well on all sides. Season with salt. Add the water and bring to the boil. Cover and simmer gently for 30 minutes. Stir in the garam masala, cover and continue cooking for a further 15 minutes or until chicken is tender. Add a little more water if the chicken becomes too dry.

CHICKEN DOPIAZAH

EASY!

Chicken cooked with spices and twice the normal amount of onions and shallots

Serves 4

30g (1 oz) ghee or butter
2 tablespoons vegetable oil
12 whole shallots, peeled
1 large onion, halved and thinly sliced
1 small onion, finely chopped
3 cloves garlic, finely chopped
3 dried red chillies, chopped
2 teaspoons chopped fresh ginger
3 teaspoons ground coriander
2 teaspoons ground cumin
½ teaspoon coarsely ground black pepper
salt
1.5 kg (3 lb) chicken, cut into 8
400g (14 oz) can chopped tomatoes and their juice
½ teaspoon ground saffron
150 ml (¼ pint) water
1 tablespoon lemon juice

1 Heat ghee and vegetable oil in a large pan and cook shallots for about 10 minutes until golden brown. Drain and set aside.

2 Add the large sliced onion and cook for about 10 minutes until golden brown. Drain and set aside.

3 Add a little more oil to the pan if necessary, and add chopped onion and cook for 5 minutes. Stir in garlic, chillies, ginger, coriander, cumin , black pepper and salt to taste. Cook for 2-3 minutes. Add the chicken and fry for about 5 minutes each side until golden brown.

4 Stir in the tomatoes, saffron and water. Bring to the

boil and cover and simmer gently for about 40 minutes until chicken is tender.

5 Scatter the cooked sliced onions and shallots on top. Cover and cook for 10 minutes. Sprinkle with lemon juice just before serving.

CHICKEN DOPIAZAH

CHICKEN DHANSAK

EASY!

Chicken pieces cooked with dhal (lentils and split peas), spices, aubergine, spinach and tomatoes.

Serves 4

250g (8 oz) mixture of red and green lentils and split peas, soaked overnight and drained
about 625 ml (1 pint) water
90-125g (3-4 oz) ghee or butter
1 large onion, chopped
3 cloves garlic, finely chopped
2 teaspoons chopped fresh ginger
4 whole cloves
4 cardamom pods
2 teaspoons garam masala
freshly ground black pepper
salt
1.5 kg (3 lb) chicken, cut into 8
1 small aubergine, chopped
500g (1 lb) fresh young spinach
400g (14 oz) can chopped tomatoes and their juice

1 Drain and rinse the dhal (lentils and split peas). Put into a saucepan with the water. Bring to the boil and simmer, covered , for about 30 minutes until soft.

2 Heat ghee in a large pan and cook onion, garlic and ginger for about 5 minutes until soft. Add cloves, cardamom, garam masala, pepper and salt and cook for 2 minutes. Add chicken pieces and cook for 5 minutes each side until lightly browned. Remove chicken from pan and drain on kitchen paper.

3 Add the aubergine, spinach and tomatoes to pan and cook for 10 minutes, stirring occasionally.

4 Mash the cooked dhal and stir into the spinach mixture. Return chicken to pan, cover and cook for about 40 minutes until chicken is tender. Add more water if necessary.

MURGH MUSSALLEM

A whole chicken marinated in yogurt and spices and then cooked in a paste made with onions and spices.

Serves 4
1.5 kg (3 lb) chicken
4 tablespoons vegetable oil
4 medium onions, chopped
2 cloves garlic, finely chopped
2 teaspoons chopped fresh ginger
1 cinnamon stick, crushed
2 dried red chillies, de-seeded and chopped
8 whole cloves
2 teaspoons cumin seeds
1 teaspoon salt
1 tablespoon ground coriander
4 small cardamoms
freshly ground black pepper
3 tablespoons lemon juice
150 ml (¼ pint) water
140g (5 oz) natural yogurt
2 tablespoons chopped fresh coriander

Marinade
4 cloves garlic
1 tablespoon finely chopped fresh ginger
1 teaspoon salt
½ teaspoon garam masala
½ teaspoon ground turmeric
¼-½ teaspoon cayenne
4 tablespoons natural yogurt

1 To make marinade, put garlic, ginger, salt, garam masala, turmeric, cayenne and yogurt into a bowl and mix well together. Prick chicken all over with a sharp fork or make small slits with a sharp knife. Rub the marinade all over the chicken, inside and out, and leave at room temperature for 1 hour or in the fridge for 2 hours.

2 Heat 2 tablespoons oil in a large pan and cook the onions, garlic and ginger until soft and just beginning to brown. Remove, drain well and put into a food processor or blender. Add cinnamon, chillies, cloves, cumin seeds, salt, coriander, cardamoms, pepper and lemon juice and blend well until smooth.

3 Heat remaining oil in a large flameproof casserole. Put the chicken and marinade into the pan and brown on all sides. Turn the heat to low. Spread the spiced onion mixture over the chicken. Mix together the water and yogurt and pour into the pan. Cover tightly. Simmer gently for about 45-50 minutes until chicken is tender. Turn the chicken regularly during cooking and baste well. Serve sprinkled with the chopped fresh coriander.

MURGH MUSSALLEM

CHICKEN TIKKA MASALA

EASY!

Pieces of chicken marinated and then grilled and served in a spicy yogurt sauce.

Serves 4-6

2 tablespoons fresh lime juice
1 teaspoon chopped fresh ginger
1 clove garlic, crushed
1 teaspoon chilli powder
2 tablespoons chopped fresh coriander
salt
freshly ground black pepper
8 small chicken breasts, skinned, boned and cubed
2 tablespoons vegetable oil
2 onions, thinly sliced
1 teaspoon turmeric
250g (8 oz) natural yogurt
1 green chilli, de-seeded and chopped

1 Put lime juice, ginger, garlic, chilli powder, half the coriander, salt and pepper into a bowl and mix well together. Add chicken and toss well. Cover and leave in a cool place overnight.

2 Thread the chicken pieces onto skewers and cook under a preheated grill for about 10-15 minutes until cooked through.

3 Meanwhile, heat oil in a frying pan and cook onion for about 10 minutes until golden brown. Add the turmeric and cook for a minute. Remove from heat and add yogurt, remaining coriander and chilli. Stir over a low heat for a few minutes until sauce thickens.

4 Remove chicken pieces from skewers and stir into yogurt. Heat for about 5 minutes and serve.

FISH AND
SEAFOOD CURRIES

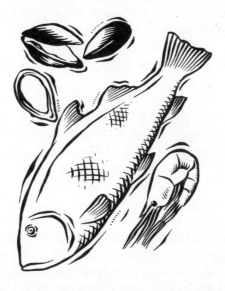

India has a large coastline and so in the neighbouring regions a great deal of fish is consumed. Many varieties of fish are caught that are not available here, but in most cases any firm white fish can be used. Some of the finest prawns come from Indian waters so it is no surprise that there are very many excellent prawn recipes. Some of the recipes below use ordinary prawns, but if you can stretch to using king or tiger prawns you will have even more delicious results.

SPICY RED PRAWNS

REALLY EASY!

**A very hot dish of prawns marinated with chillies,
then quickly stir-fried and finally cooked in a dish
in the oven with tomatoes and coriander.**

Serves 2-3

16 large uncooked prawns, peeled and deveined
3 large tomatoes, peeled, de-seeded and chopped
1 tablespoon vegetable oil
2 tablespoons chopped fresh coriander

Marinade
6 cloves garlic, finely chopped
2 teaspoons finely chopped fresh ginger
8 fresh red or green chillies, finely chopped
3 tablespoons lemon juice
1 tablespoon caster sugar
salt

1 To make marinade, place garlic, ginger, chillies, lemon juice, sugar and salt to taste in a bowl and mix to combine. Add prawns and toss to coat with marinade. Cover and marinate in the refrigerator for 15-20 hours.

2 Place tomatoes in a food processor or blender and process until smooth.

3 Preheat the oven to 160C,325F,Gas 3. Heat oil in a wok or large frying pan, reduce heat to low, add prawns and marinade and cook, stirring constantly, for 2-3 minutes until prawns turn pink. Transfer prawns to a casserole dish, add tomatoes and coriander and mix well to combine. Cover and bake in preheated oven for 30 minutes.

TANDOORI FISH

R E A L L Y   E A S Y !

**Fillets of fish spread with a mixture of yogurt,
garlic and spices and quickly cooked
under the grill.**

Serves 4
*170g (6 oz) natural yogurt
1 teaspoon minced or finely chopped garlic
1 teaspoon ground cumin
¼ teaspoon chilli powder
¼ teaspoon ground turmeric
4 fish cutlets or fillets, such as cod, halibut, salmon or
mackerel*

1 Preheat the grill. Place yogurt, garlic, cumin, chilli and turmeric in a bowl and mix to combine. Spread each cutlet or fillet with yogurt mixture on one side.

2 Place fish under a preheated grill and cook for 3-4 minutes. Carefully turn the fish over and spread with remaining yogurt mixture. Cook for a further 2-3 minutes until fish is tender.

SPICY RED PRAWNS • TANDOORI FISH

BAKED FISH

EASY!

White fish fillets baked in the oven with a sauce made from onion purée, tomatoes, spices and cream.

Serves 4

2 large onions, roughly chopped
1 tablespoon vegetable oil
2 cloves garlic, crushed
2 fresh red or green chillies, finely chopped
2 teaspoons finely chopped fresh ginger
1 tablespoon cumin seeds
2 bay leaves
salt
4 large tomatoes, skinned and finely chopped
½ teaspoon ground cumin
½ teaspoon ground coriander
pinch ground cloves
pinch ground cinnamon
pinch ground cardamom
½ teaspoon mango powder
¼ teaspoon ground turmeric
3 tablespoons double cream
4 firm white fish fillets, such as cod or halibut
2 tablespoons chopped fresh basil

1 Preheat oven to 180C, 350F, Gas 4. Place onions in a food processor or blender and process to make a purée.

2 Heat oil in a heavy-based saucepan, add garlic, chillies, ginger, cumin seeds, bay leaves, salt to taste and onion purée and cook over a medium heat until onions are a pinkish colour. Add tomatoes, ground cumin, coriander, cloves, cinnamon, cardamom, mango powder and turmeric and cook, stirring, for 3-4 minutes. Remove pan from heat and stir in cream.

3 Place fish in a baking dish, pour over sauce and bake in the preheated oven for 20 minutes or until fish flakes when tested with a fork. Just prior to serving, sprinkle with basil.

PRAWN PATIA

E A S Y !

**Prawns cooked in a thick sweet sour coating
of tamarind, sugar, vinegar, tomato
purée and spices.**

Serves 4

2 tablespoons vegetable oil
1 onion, chopped
2 cloves garlic, finely chopped
2 teaspoons chopped fresh ginger
1 teaspoon cumin seeds
½ teaspoon mustard seeds
½ teaspoon fennel seeds
½ teaspoon fenugreek seeds
½ teaspoon ground turmeric
1 teaspoon paprika
1 teaspoon ground coriander
4 tablespoons coconut milk
½-1 tablespoon tamarind concentrate
1 tablespoon brown sugar
1 tablespoon clear honey
1 tablespoon white vinegar
1 tablespoon tomato purée
500g (1 lb) cooked peeled prawns

1 Heat oil in a pan and fry onion, garlic, ginger, cumin seeds, mustard seeds, fennel seeds and fenugreek seeds for about 10 minutes until onion is soft.

2 Stir in the turmeric, paprika and coriander and cook for a minute. Add the coconut milk, tamarind concentrate, brown sugar, honey, vinegar and tomato purée and stir well. Add the prawns and cook gently for 10 minutes until prawns are heated through and well-coated in sauce.

PRAWN MADRAS

REALLY EASY!

**Prawns cooked in a very hot spicy mixture of
chilli, curry spices, coconut and tomatoes.**

Serves 4

1 tablespoon vegetable oil
1 onion, finely chopped
2 cloves garlic, finely chopped
1 teaspoon chilli powder
1 teaspoon ground coriander
½ teaspoon ground cumin
½ teaspoon mustard powder
½ teaspoon ground fenugreek
¼ teaspoon ground turmeric
2 tablespoons desiccated coconut
5-6 dried curry leaves
225g (8 oz) can chopped tomatoes and their juice
1 green chilli, finely chopped
500g (1 lb) cooked peeled prawns
1 tablespoon chopped fresh coriander

1 Heat oil in a pan and fry onion until lightly browned.
Add garlic, chilli powder, ground coriander, cumin,
mustard powder, fenugreek and turmeric and cook for a
minute.

2 Stir in coconut, curry leaves, tomatoes and chilli. Add
the prawns and cook for 10 minutes. Serve sprinkled with
chopped coriander.

BALTI KING PRAWNS

EASY!

Balti dishes take their name from the dish in which they are brought to the table. The balti pan is like a wok and the prawns are stir-fried quickly with onion and then a previously made spicy sauce is poured on top and the whole thing cooked until piping hot.

Serves 4

4 tablespoons vegetable oil
2 onions, chopped
2 cloves garlic, chopped
1 tablespoon finely chopped ginger
2 green chillies, chopped
seeds from 5 green cardamom pods
¼ teaspoon ground cloves
1 teaspoon ground coriander
1 teaspoon paprika
1 teaspoon ground cinnamon
1 teaspoon ground turmeric
½ teaspoon ground cumin
¼ teaspoon ground fenugreek
½ teaspoon mustard powder
225g (8 oz) can chopped tomatoes and their juice
250 ml (8 fl oz) stock
1 tablespoon lemon juice
500g (1 lb) uncooked king or tiger prawns, peeled and deveined
60g (2 oz) creamed coconut
30g (1 oz) ground almonds
60g (2 oz) flaked toasted almonds

1 Heat 2 tablespoons of oil in a pan and add half the onions, the garlic and ginger and cook for 5 minutes. Add chillies and cook for a minute. Stir in cardamom, cloves, coriander, paprika, cinnamon, turmeric, cumin, fenugreek, and mustard powder and cook for a minute. Add tomatoes and stock and simmer uncovered for 30 minutes. Remove from heat and add lemon juice.

2 Heat remaining oil in a large balti pan, frying pan or wok and cook remaining chopped onion for 2-3 minutes over a high heat. Stir in prawns and cook for 2-3 minutes until they turn pink.

3 Add the prepared sauce, coconut and ground almonds and cook gently for 10 minutes until prawns are cooked through. Sprinkle with toasted almonds and serve.

BALTI KING PRAWNS

BHUNA PRAWNS

REALLY EASY!

Bhuna dishes are dry with very little or no sauce. In this dish the prawns are marinated in spices with lemon juice before frying with onion and a little water to stop them from sticking.

Serves 4

1½ teaspoons garam masala
1-2 teaspoons chilli powder
½ teaspoon ground turmeric
2 cloves garlic, finely chopped
2 tablespoons lemon juice
500g (1 lb) cooked peeled prawns
2 tablespoons vegetable oil
1 onion, chopped
about 150 ml (¼ pint) water
1 fresh green chilli, de-seeded and very thinly sliced
1 tablespoon chopped fresh coriander

1 Put garam masala, chilli powder, turmeric, garlic and lemon juice into a bowl. Add prawns and mix well together and leave to marinate for 15 minutes.

2 Heat oil in a pan and cook onion gently for about 10 minutes until golden brown. Add the prawns and marinade and the water and cook for a further 10 minutes until prawns are heated through and most of the water has evaporated. Stir well whilst cooking. Sprinkle with sliced chilli and coriander before serving.

VEGETARIAN CURRIES

Many Indians are vegetarian and there are a
great variety of vegetable and vegetarian dishes
in their cuisine. Popular vegetables to use are
potatoes, aubergine, peas, cauliflower and
tomatoes. In some recipes, protein is added in
the form of eggs, soft cheese (panir), lentils or
nuts. As well as this section, vegetarian dishes
can be found in the chapters on Vegetables,
Dhals, and Rice.

COCONUT VEGETABLE CURRY

REALLY EASY!

Potatoes, aubergine, courgettes and red pepper cooked with tomatoes, spices and coconut milk.

Serves 4
1 tablespoon vegetable oil
1 onion, chopped
2 cloves garlic, crushed
1 teaspoon ground cumin
1 teaspoon ground coriander
1 teaspoon garam masala
½ teaspoon chilli powder
2 tablespoons flour
250 ml (8 fl oz) vegetable stock or water
400g (14 oz) canned tomatoes, undrained and mashed
2 large potatoes, chopped
1 aubergine, chopped
2 courgettes, chopped
1 red pepper, chopped
125 ml (4 fl oz) coconut milk

1 Heat oil in a large frying pan, add onion and stir-fry for 5 minutes or until onion is soft. Add garlic, cumin, coriander, garam masala, chilli powder and flour and cook, stirring, for 1 minute.

2 Stir in stock or water, tomatoes and potatoes and bring to the boil. Reduce heat, cover and simmer for 15 minutes. Add aubergine , courgettes and red pepper and cook for 10 minutes or until vegetables are tender. Stir in coconut milk and cook, stirring, for 5 minutes or until heated through.

PUMPKIN AND RED LENTIL STEW

EASY!

Cubes of pumpkin in a spicy tomato sauce with lentils. Be careful not to overcook pumpkin or it will collapse and turn mushy. Instead of pumpkin you can use a mixture of potatoes and extra carrots.

Serves 4

2 tablespoons vegetable oil
1 onion, chopped
1 clove garlic, crushed
1 teaspoon ground cumin
1 teaspoon ground coriander
1 teaspoon ground turmeric
2 carrots, peeled and sliced
125g (4 oz) red lentils
400g (14 oz) canned tomatoes, undrained
375 ml (12 fl oz) vegetable stock
1-2 teaspoons chilli sauce, according to taste
500g (1 lb) pumpkin, peeled and cut into 2.5 cm (1 inch) cubes
freshly ground black pepper
natural yogurt to serve

1 Heat oil in a large saucepan and cook onion, garlic, cumin, coriander, turmeric and carrots for 5 minutes or until onion softens.

2 Stir in lentils, tomatoes and stock and bring to the boil. Reduce heat, cover and simmer for 15 minutes.

3 Add chilli sauce and pumpkin and cook for 15-20 minutes or until pumpkin is tender. Season to taste with pepper. Ladle stew into bowls and top with a spoonful of yogurt.

COCONUT VEGETABLE CURRY • PUMPKIN AND RED LENTIL STEW

79

COCONUT CURRIED EGGS

REALLY EASY!

Sliced hard-boiled eggs in a quick curry sauce made with butter, cornflour, curry powder, chicken stock and coconut milk.

Serves 4
8 hard-boiled eggs, each one thickly sliced into 4

Coconut Curry Sauce
30g (1 oz) butter
1 onion, chopped
2 teaspoons curry powder
1 teaspoon ground cumin
1 tablespoon cornflour
250 ml (8 fl oz) chicken stock
250 ml (8 fl oz) coconut milk
2 tablespoons lemon juice

1 Preheat the oven to 180C, 350F, Gas 4. To make sauce, melt butter in a saucepan and cook onion for 3-4 minutes or until soft. Stir in curry powder, cumin and cornflour, and cook for 1 minute longer.

2 Place stock, coconut milk and lemon juice in a bowl and mix to combine. Stir stock mixture into pan and cook over a medium heat, stirring constantly, for 4-5 minutes or until sauce boils and thickens.

3 Place eggs in a large ovenproof dish, pour curry sauce over and bake in the preheated oven for 10-15 minutes or until heated through.

POTATO CURRY

E A S Y !

A mild curry of potatoes, onions, aubergine, peas and tomatoes, cooked with coconut milk and a dash of lemon juice.

Serves 4
2 tablespoons vegetable oil
2 onions, sliced
1 teaspoon minced or finely chopped garlic
1 small aubergine, cubed
2 large potatoes, cubed
400g (14 oz) canned tomatoes, drained and chopped
90g (3 oz) frozen peas
1 tablespoon tomato purée
1 tablespoon mild curry powder
2 teaspoons ground cumin
2 teaspoons ground coriander
250 ml (8 fl oz) coconut milk
1 tablespoon lemon juice

1 Heat oil in a large frying pan and cook onions, garlic, aubergine and potatoes over a medium heat, stirring constantly, for 2 minutes.

2 Stir in tomatoes, peas, tomato purée, curry powder, cumin, coriander and coconut milk, bring just to the boil and simmer for 15 minutes or until vegetables are tender. Stir in lemon juice and serve with rice and a salad.

PANIR WITH TOMATO SAUCE

E A S Y !

**Panir is a fresh cheese made with curdled milk
which is readily available in India in grocery
stores. It is, however, very easy to make and in
this recipe the panir is added to a mixture of
spices, chilli and tomato.**

Serves 3-4

Panir
*2 litres (3½ pints) milk
170g (6 oz) natural yogurt
2 tablespoons lemon juice
salt*

Tomato Sauce
*1 tablespoon vegetable oil
2 teaspoons finely chopped fresh ginger
1 fresh red or green chilli, finely chopped
1 teaspoon cumin seeds
2 large tomatoes, skinned and chopped
¼ teaspoon ground cumin
¼ teaspoon ground coriander
pinch ground turmeric
pinch mango powder
2-3 tablespoons chopped fresh coriander*

1 To make panir, place milk in a saucepan and bring to
the boil over a low heat. Stir in yogurt, lemon juice and
salt to taste, then remove from heat. Stand for 2 minutes
to allow the curds and whey to separate. Line a colander
with muslin or cheesecloth and set colander over a bowl.
Pour milk mixture into colander and set aside to drain
overnight.

2 To make sauce, heat oil in a non-stick frying pan, add ginger, chilli, cumin seeds and tomatoes and cook, stirring, for 2 minutes. Add panir, ground cumin, ground coriander, turmeric and mango powder and mix well to combine. Just prior to serving, sprinkle with fresh coriander. Serve with Indian bread.

VEGETABLE PULLAO

EASY!

**A pilau made with rice and a selection of
diced vegetables, spices, and chillies, and
garnished with tomatoes, hard-boiled eggs,
cashews and sultanas.**

Serves 4

*500g (1 lb) mixed vegetables such as peas, diced
potatoes, sliced beans, diced courgette, diced carrot and
cauliflower florets
2 tablespoons vegetable oil
1 onion, sliced
1 bay leaf
1 cinnamon stick
½ teaspoon fennel seeds
½ teaspoon cumin seeds
½ teaspoon black mustard seeds
½ teaspoon yellow mustard seeds
¼ teaspoon fenugreek seeds
2 teaspoons finely chopped fresh ginger
2 fresh red or green chillies, finely chopped
400g (14 oz) basmati rice
1.2 litres (2 pints) hot water
2 hard-boiled eggs, sliced
2 tomatoes, sliced
60g (2 oz) salted cashew nuts, roughly chopped
90g (3 oz) sultanas*

1 Boil, steam or microwave vegetables until partially
cooked. Drain and set aside.

2 Preheat oven to 180C, 350F, Gas 4. Heat oil in a large
saucepan, add onion, bay leaf, cinnamon stick, fennel
seeds, cumin seeds, black mustard seeds, yellow mustard
seeds, fenugreek seeds, ginger and chillies and cook over
a medium heat for 1 minute.

3 Stir in rice and mix well to combine. Add mixed vegetables and cook for 2 minutes. Stir in hot water and transfer rice mixture to a casserole dish. Cover and bake in the preheated oven for 20-30 minutes or until rice is cooked.

4 Place rice mixture on a large serving platter. Decorate border with alternating slices of egg and tomato, then sprinkle with cashews and sultanas.

INDIAN EGG CURRY

EASY!

Hard-boiled eggs coated with a Curry Sauce made with onion, spices, tomatoes and coconut milk.

Serves 4
6 hard-boiled eggs, halved lengthwise

Curry Sauce
1 tablespoon vegetable oil
1 large onion, finely chopped
1 clove garlic, crushed
1 tablespoon finely chopped fresh ginger
1 teaspoon ground cumin
1 teaspoon ground coriander
½ teaspoon chilli powder
1 teaspoon ground turmeric
400g (14 oz) canned tomatoes, undrained and mashed
125 ml (4 fl oz) coconut milk
freshly ground black pepper

1 Preheat oven to 180C,350F,Gas 4. To make sauce, heat oil in a frying pan and cook onion, garlic and ginger over a medium heat for 5 minutes or until onion softens. Stir in cumin, coriander, chilli powder and turmeric, and cook for 2 minutes longer.

2 Add tomatoes and coconut milk, bring to the boil, then reduce heat and simmer for 15 minutes or until sauce reduces and thickens. Season to taste with black pepper.

3 Place eggs in a shallow baking dish and spoon sauce over. Cover and bake in the preheated oven for 20 minutes or until heated through.

VEGETABLE KORMA

REALLY EASY!

A tasty dish of onions, curry paste, ginger and chilli with tomatoes, green beans, cauliflower, broccoli, and red and green peppers. Fresh mint and cashew nuts are stirred in before serving. You can vary the vegetables in this tasty stew and use whatever is in season.

Serves 6

1 tablespoon vegetable oil
2 onions, cut into eighths
1 tablespoon curry paste
1 clove garlic, crushed
1 tablespoon grated fresh ginger
1 teaspoon chilli powder
400g (14 oz) canned tomatoes, undrained and mashed
200g (7 oz) green beans, trimmed and halved
250g (8 oz) cauliflower, broken into small florets
250g (8 oz) broccoli, broken into small florets
1 red pepper, chopped
1 green pepper, chopped
2 tablespoons chopped fresh mint
200g (7 oz) unsalted roasted cashew nuts

1 Heat oil in a large saucepan over a medium heat. Add onions, curry paste, garlic, ginger and chilli powder and cook, stirring, for 3 minutes or until onions are soft.

2 Add tomatoes, beans, cauliflower, broccoli, red pepper and green pepper and cook, stirring occasionally, for about 10 minutes or until vegetables are tender. Stir in the mint and cashew nuts and serve.

INDIAN EGG CURRY • VEGETABLE KORMA

VEGETABLE CURRY WITH CHUTNEY

EASY!

Onions, potatoes, cauliflower, broccoli, green beans, red pepper and courgettes cooked with stock and coconut milk until tender and served with Rhubarb Chutney.

Serves 4

Rhubarb Chutney
500g (1 lb) rhubarb, chopped
1 tablespoon grated fresh ginger
1 fresh green chilli, chopped
1 tablespoon black mustard seeds
125g (4 oz) brown sugar
250 ml (8 fl oz) white vinegar
60g (2 oz) currants

Vegetable Curry
1 tablespoon vegetable oil
1 teaspoon ground cumin
1 tablespoon curry paste
2 onions, chopped
2 medium potatoes, finely chopped
200g (7 oz) cauliflower cut into florets
200g (7 oz) broccoli, cut into florets
150g (5 oz) green beans, halved
1 red pepper, chopped
2 courgettes, chopped
200 ml (7 fl oz) coconut milk
200 ml (7 fl oz) vegetable stock

1 To make chutney, place rhubarb, ginger, chilli, mustard seeds, sugar, vinegar and currants in a saucepan and cook over a medium heat, stirring occasionally, for 30 minutes or until mixture is soft and pulpy.

2 To make curry, heat oil in a large saucepan, add cumin, curry paste and onions and cook, stirring, for 3 minutes or until onions are soft. Add potatoes, cauliflower, broccoli, beans, red pepper, courgettes, coconut milk and stock and bring to the boil. Reduce heat and simmer, stirring occasionally, for about 25 minutes or until vegetables are tender. Serve curry with Rhubarb Chutney.

VEGETABLE CURRY WITH CHUTNEY

SALADS

Indian salads are usually very simple and use just a few ingredients, generally tossed with a lemon-juice-based dressing. They are often served as a starter with poppadums, but they make a refreshing contrast and addition to main meal dishes. In this chapter you will find Tomato and Onion Salad, which is a variation on the popular Onion Salad found in many Indian restaurants, plus others such as Carrot and Mandarin, and Cucumber and Mint, that are equally good to eat and very easy to make.

CUCUMBER, MINT AND BASIL SALAD

REALLY EASY!

Diced cucumber with chillies, fresh mint and basil, tossed in a Lemon and Spice Dressing.

Serves 4
1 cucumber, diced
2 tablespoons chopped fresh mint
2 tablespoons chopped fresh basil
2 small fresh red or green chillies, finely chopped

Lemon And Spice Dressing
1-2 tablespoons lemon juice
pinch mango powder
pinch paprika
pinch salt

1 Place cucumber, mint, basil and chillies in a salad bowl.

2 To make dressing, put lemon juice, mango powder, paprika and salt in a small bowl and mix well to combine. Pour dressing over salad and toss together.

LETTUCE AND DILL SALAD

REALLY EASY!

Shredded lettuce and finely sliced cucumber, flavoured with dill and lemon juice.

Serves 4-6
½ lettuce, shredded
½ large cucumber, peeled and thinly sliced
2 tablespoons chopped fresh dill
2 tablespoons lemon juice
pinch paprika
salt

1 Place lettuce, cucumber, dill, lemon juice, paprika and salt to taste in a salad bowl and toss to combine.

TOMATO AND ONION SALAD

REALLY EASY!

Thin slices of onion and tomato, dressed with lemon juice and fresh coriander.

Serves 4
1 onion, thinly sliced
2 tomatoes, thinly sliced
salt
2 tablespoons lemon juice
1 tablespoon chopped fresh coriander

1 Place onion, tomato and salt to taste in a bowl, pour over lemon juice and sprinkle with coriander. Toss to combine and serve.

FRESH GREEN VEGETABLE SALAD

REALLY EASY!

An unusual mix of lettuce, cucumber, avocado, celery and bean sprouts, dressed with spiced lemon juice.

Serves 4-6
½ head lettuce, leaves separated
½ cucumber, peeled and sliced
1 avocado, stoned, peeled and sliced
2 stalks celery, sliced
125g (4 oz) bean sprouts

Lemon Dressing
2 tablespoons lemon juice
½ teaspoon paprika
½ teaspoon mango powder
½ teaspoon caster sugar
salt
freshly ground black pepper

1 Place lettuce, cucumber, avocado, celery and bean sprouts in a salad bowl.

2 To make dressing, put lemon juice, paprika, mango powder, sugar, and salt and black pepper to taste in a small bowl and mix well to combine. Spoon dressing over salad and toss together.

LETTUCE & DILL • TOMATO & ONION • FRESH GREEN VEGETABLE

CARROT AND MANDARIN SALAD

EASY!

**A brightly coloured salad of grated carrot
with mint and mandarin segments
and lemon dressing.**

Serves 4-6

2 mandarins, segmented, all pith removed
2 large carrots, grated
2 tablespoons chopped fresh mint
2 tablespoons lemon juice
¼ teaspoon paprika
¼ teaspoon mango powder
½ teaspoon caster sugar
salt
freshly ground black pepper

1 Slice each mandarin segment in half from outside edge to centre, making sure not to cut right through. Open each segment to form a circle and remove seeds. Arrange mandarin segments attractively on a serving platter.

2 Top mandarins with grated carrots and sprinkle with chopped mint. Put lemon juice, paprika, mango powder, sugar, and salt and black pepper to taste in a small bowl and mix well to combine. Spoon lemon juice mixture over salad and serve.

CABBAGE SALAD

E A S Y !

Crunchy cabbage flavoured with lemon juice and fresh coriander.

Serves 4

½ small white cabbage, finely shredded
1 tablespoon lemon juice
pinch paprika
pinch caster sugar
pinch salt
freshly ground black pepper
2 tablespoons chopped fresh coriander.

1 Place cabbage in a flat bowl or dish.

2 Put lemon juice, paprika, sugar, salt and black pepper to taste in a small bowl and mix well. Just prior to serving, spoon dressing over cabbage and toss to combine. Sprinkle with coriander and serve.

CARROT AND MANDARIN SALAD • CABBAGE SALAD

DELHI SALAD

REALLY EASY!

A refreshing mixture of diced cucumbers, radishes, potatoes and tomatoes, flavoured with chilli and coriander, and tossed in a creamy spice dressing.

Serves 6

90 ml (3 fl oz) light sesame seed or light vegetable oil
90 ml (3 fl oz) double cream
3 tablespoons lemon juice
½ teaspoon garlic, finely chopped
½ teaspoon finely chopped ginger
¼ teaspoon ground cumin
2 teaspoons caster sugar
salt
2 small cucumbers, diced
4 radishes, diced
5 small potatoes, cooked and diced
2 fresh green chillies, chopped
2-3 tablespoons chopped fresh coriander
3 tomatoes, chopped

1 Place oil, cream, lemon juice, garlic, ginger, cumin, sugar and salt to taste in a bowl and whisk to combine. Cover and refrigerate for 20 minutes before serving.

2 Place cucumbers, radishes, potatoes, chillies, coriander and tomatoes in a bowl. Spoon over the dressing and toss to combine.

MOGUL SALAD

REALLY EASY

A salad of bean sprouts, cucumbers and tomatoes, flavoured with coconut, fresh herbs and spring onions, and tossed in lemon juice.

Serves 6

200g (7 oz) bean sprouts
3 small cucumbers, diced
1 tablespoon grated fresh or desiccated coconut
2 tomatoes, diced
1 tablespoon chopped fresh coriander
2 tablespoons chopped fresh mint
2 tablespoons chopped fresh basil
6 spring onions, chopped
2 tablespoons lemon juice
salt
freshly ground black pepper

1 Place bean sprouts, cucumbers, coconut, tomatoes, coriander, mint, basil, spring onions, lemon juice, and salt and black pepper to taste in a bowl and toss to combine. Cover and stand at room temperature for 1 hour before serving.

VEGETABLES

Indian vegetables dishes are often cooked 'dry', that is with only natural juices or a little water supplying the moisture. So that the delicate flavour of the vegetable is not overpowered, only small amounts of spices are used. Coriander and chillies are much used as flavourings and chillies should always be used cautiously as they vary in strength.

OKRA CURRY

REALLY EASY!

**Small pieces of okra cooked with onion, garlic
and spices and a little tomato sauce to moisten.
In this dish you can, if you like, replace the
okra with courgettes.**

Serves 4

*2 tablespoons vegetable oil
1 onion, thinly sliced
1 clove garlic, thinly sliced
1 teaspoon ground coriander
½ teaspoon ground turmeric
½ teaspoon chilli powder
1 teaspoon garam masala
500g (1 lb) fresh okra, topped, tailed and cut into 1 cm
(½ inch) pieces
2 tablespoons tomato sauce*

1 Heat oil in a saucepan. Cook onion and garlic for 5
minutes. Stir in coriander, turmeric, chilli powder and
garam masala. Cook for 1-2 minutes, stirring frequently
during cooking.

2 Add okra and stir gently to coat with the spices. Cook
for 5 minutes. Blend in tomato sauce. If curry is too dry,
add a little boiling water. Cover and cook gently until
okra is soft.

SPICY VEGETABLES

EASY!

**A selection of freshly cooked vegetables tossed
in a dry spice mixture, with chillies, tomatoes
and lemon juice.**

Serves 4
250g (8 oz) baby new potatoes, diced
½ small cauliflower, broken into florets
250g (8 oz) fresh or frozen peas
2 tablespoons vegetable oil
3 small onions, finely chopped
2 teaspoons finely chopped fresh ginger
4 cloves garlic, finely chopped
1 fresh red or green chilli, finely chopped
1 teaspoon cumin seeds
salt
2 tomatoes, diced
60 ml (2 fl oz) lemon juice
2-3 tablespoons chopped fresh coriander

Dry Spice Mixture
1 teaspoon ground cumin
1 teaspoon ground coriander
½ teaspoon ground cinnamon
½ teaspoon ground turmeric
¼ teaspoon ground fennel
¼ teaspoon cayenne pepper
¼ teaspoon mango powder
¼ teaspoon ground bay leaves

1 Boil or microwave potatoes, cauliflower and peas,
separately, until tender. Drain and set aside.

2 For spice mixture, place cumin, coriander, cinnamon,
turmeric, fennel, cayenne pepper, mango powder and
bay leaves in a bowl and mix to combine. Set aside.

3 Heat oil in a large heavy-based saucepan, add onions, ginger, garlic, chilli, cumin seeds and salt to taste and cook over a low heat, stirring occasionally, for 10-15 minutes or until onions are soft and transparent. Add tomatoes and cook, stirring occasionally, for 10 minutes or until tomatoes are soft and pulpy. Add spice mixture and simmer, stirring constantly, for 2 minutes. Add cooked vegetables and lemon juice and cook, stirring occasionally, for 5-10 minutes or until vegetables are heated through. Just prior to serving, stir in chopped coriander.

SPICY VEGETABLES

CAULIFLOWER KHEEMA

REALLY EASY!

A spicy dish of finely chopped cauliflower with onions, tomatoes, chilli and ginger. Butternut squash is also delicious when cooked in this way.

Serves 6

1 tablespoon vegetable oil
2 teaspoons finely chopped fresh ginger
2 fresh red or green chillies, finely chopped
2 teaspoons cumin seeds
2 bay leaves
salt
2 large onions
1 cauliflower, cut into small florets and very finely chopped
125 ml (4 fl oz) water
4 large tomatoes, skinned and finely chopped
1 teaspoon ground coriander
1 teaspoon ground cumin
1 teaspoon garam masala
1 teaspoon mango powder
½ teaspoon ground turmeric

1 Heat oil in a heavy-based saucepan over a low heat. Add ginger, chillies, cumin seeds, bay leaves and salt to taste and cook, stirring, for 1 minute.

2 Place onions in a food processor or blender and process until almost puréed. Add onions to pan and cook, stirring frequently, for 12-15 minutes or until onions are golden. Add cauliflower and water and cook, stirring, for 5-6 minutes or until cauliflower is tender.

3 Add tomatoes and cook, stirring occasionally, for 10 minutes. Stir in coriander, ground cumin, garam masala, mango powder and turmeric and cook for 5 minutes.

SPICY TOMATOES

REALLY EASY!

Chopped tomatoes cooked with ginger, chillies, spices and lots of fresh coriander.

Serves 6

2 tablespoons vegetable oil
2 large onions, chopped
1 teaspoon cumin seeds
2 teaspoons finely chopped fresh ginger
2 fresh red or green chillies, chopped
salt
6 large tomatoes, peeled and chopped
1 teaspoon ground cumin
1 teaspoon ground coriander
½ teaspoon mango powder
¼ teaspoon ground turmeric
4 tablespoons chopped fresh coriander

1 Heat oil in a heavy-based saucepan, add onions, cumin seeds, ginger, chillies and salt to taste. Cook, stirring frequently, for 10 minutes or until onions are a light golden colour.

2 Stir in tomatoes and cook for 5-7 minutes. Stir in ground cumin, ground coriander, mango powder, turmeric and fresh coriander and cook for 2 minutes longer.

CAULIFLOWER KHEEMA • SPICY TOMATOES

AUBERGINES WITH TOMATOES

EASY!

Baby aubergines halved and cooked, and then topped with a hot spicy mixture of onion, garlic, chilli and tomato.

Serves 6
12 baby aubergines
4 tablespoons vegetable oil
2 onions, chopped
2 fresh red or green chillies, finely chopped
2 cloves garlic, finely chopped
2 teaspoons finely chopped fresh ginger
3 tomatoes, skinned and chopped
1 tablespoon lemon juice
¼ teaspoon ground paprika
¼ teaspoon ground cardamom
½ teaspoon ground cumin
½ teaspoon ground coriander
½ teaspoon mango powder
¼ teaspoon ground turmeric
2 tablespoons chopped fresh coriander

1 Trim ends from aubergines and split lengthwise. Heat 2 tablespoons oil in a large frying pan, add aubergines and cook, turning frequently, until they start to soften. Remove aubergines from pan and drain on absorbent kitchen paper. Set aside and keep warm.

2 Heat remaining oil in same frying pan, add onions, chillies, garlic and ginger and cook over a medium heat, stirring, for 5 minutes or until onions are golden. Stir in tomatoes, reduce heat to low and cook for 10 minutes or until tomatoes are soft and pulpy. Stir in lemon juice, paprika, cardamom, cumin, ground coriander, mango powder and turmeric and cook for 2 minutes longer. Stir in coriander.

3 To serve, spoon tomato mixture over aubergines.

DICED POTATO WITH FENUGREEK

REALLY EASY!

Potatoes cut into dice and 'dry cooked' with spices, chillies, fenugreek and fresh coriander.

Serves 4
2 tablespoons vegetable oil
½ teaspoon cumin seeds
½ teaspoon yellow mustard seeds
2 teaspoons finely chopped fresh ginger
3 fresh red or green chillies, finely chopped
salt
350g (12 oz) diced potatoes
125 ml (4 fl oz) water
2-3 tablespoons dried fenugreek leaves, washed and
drained or 1 teaspoon ground fenugreek
¼ teaspoon ground cumin
¼ teaspoon ground coriander
¼ teaspoon ground turmeric
¼ teaspoon mango powder
2 tablespoons finely chopped fresh coriander

1 Heat oil, cumin seeds, yellow mustard seeds, ginger, chillies and salt to taste in a heavy-based saucepan. Add potatoes and cook over a medium heat, stirring constantly, for 5 minutes. Add water, cover and cook over a low heat for 5 minutes or until potatoes are half-cooked.

2 Stir in fenugreek leaves, ground cumin, ground coriander, turmeric and mango powder and cook for 5-10 minutes or until potatoes are cooked. Just prior to serving, sprinkle with fresh coriander.

SPICED PEAS AND CARROTS

REALLY EASY!

Cooked peas and carrots quickly reheated in hot oil with ginger, chillies and a Dry Spice Mixture.

Serves 4

250g (8 oz) frozen or shelled peas
2 carrots, diced
2 tablespoons vegetable oil
1 teaspoon cumin seeds
2 teaspoons finely chopped fresh ginger
2 fresh red or green chillies, finely chopped
5-6 tablespoons water
salt

Dry Spice Mixture
¼ teaspoon ground cumin
¼ teaspoon ground coriander
¼ teaspoon mango powder
¼ teaspoon ground turmeric

1 For spice mixture, place cumin, coriander, mango powder and turmeric in a small bowl, mix to combine and set aside.

2 Boil or microwave peas and carrots, separately, until just cooked. Drain, refresh under cold running water and set aside. Heat oil in a heavy-based saucepan over a low heat, add cumin seeds, ginger and chillies and cook, stirring, for 2-3 minutes. Add peas and carrots and mix to combine well. Stir in water and salt to taste and simmer for 5 minutes. Add spice mixture and simmer, stirring occasionally, for 5 minutes longer.

DICED POTATO WITH FENUGREEK • SPICED PEAS AND CARROTS

CAULIFLOWER WITH BUTTERNUT SQUASH SAUCE

EASY!

Butternut squash puréed with spices and then used to coat cooked cauliflower florets, sprinkled with fresh coriander and baked in the oven.

Serves 4

1 cauliflower, broken into florets, stems removed
1 butternut squash, grated
2 tablespoons vegetable oil
60 ml (2 fl oz) water
¼ teaspoon ground cumin
¼ teaspoon ground coriander
¼ teaspoon ground turmeric
¼ teaspoon mango powder
2 teaspoons finely chopped fresh ginger
2 fresh red or green chillies, finely chopped
salt
2 tablespoons finely chopped fresh coriander

1 Steam or microwave cauliflower and squash, separately, until just tender. Drain cauliflower and refresh under cold water and set aside. Drain squash, place in a food processor or blender and process to form a purée. Set aside.

2 Heat 1 tablespoon oil in a wok or large frying pan, add cauliflower, water, cumin, ground coriander, turmeric and mango powder and cook, stirring frequently, for 5-7 minutes. Transfer cauliflower mixture to an ovenproof dish and set aside.

3 Preheat the oven to 150C,300F,Gas 2. Heat remaining oil in a saucepan, add ginger and chillies and cook, stirring, for 1 minute. Add squash purée and cook over a low heat for 5 minutes. Season to taste with salt. Pour sauce mixture over cauliflower, sprinkle with fresh coriander and bake for 30 minutes.

CAULIFLOWER WITH BUTTERNUT SQUASH SAUCE

BEAN SPROUTS WITH SPINACH

REALLY EASY!

Bean sprouts and spinach leaves very quickly cooked with ginger, chillies and spices. This dish should be made just prior to serving.

Serves 6
1 tablespoon vegetable oil
1 teaspoon finely chopped fresh ginger
2 fresh red or green chillies, finely chopped
1 teaspoon cumin seeds
1 teaspoon yellow mustard seeds
200g (7 oz) fresh bean sprouts
2 tablespoons water
1.5 kg (3 lb) young spinach leaves, chopped
½ teaspoon ground turmeric
2 teaspoons lemon juice
salt

1 Heat oil in a wok or large frying pan, add ginger, chillies, cumin seeds and yellow mustard seeds and cook over a low heat, stirring, for 2-3 minutes.

2 Add bean sprouts and water and cook, stirring, for 5 minutes. Add spinach, turmeric, lemon juice and salt to taste and cook, stirring, for 5 minutes longer. Serve immediately.

PEAS AND POTATOES

REALLY EASY!

Diced potatoes cooked with cumin, ginger and chillies until tender and then mixed with tomatoes, peas, spices and fresh coriander and simmered gently.

Serves 6
1 tablespoon vegetable oil
2 teaspoons cumin seeds
2 teaspoons finely chopped fresh ginger
2 fresh red or green chillies, finely chopped
4 large potatoes, diced
salt
4 tomatoes, skinned and diced
250g (8 oz) fresh or frozen peas, boiled, cooking water reserved
½ teaspoon mango powder
½ teaspoon ground turmeric
1 teaspoon ground cumin
1 teaspoon ground coriander
2 teaspoons chopped fresh coriander

1 Heat oil in a heavy-based saucepan over a low heat, add cumin seeds, ginger, chillies, potatoes and salt to taste and cook, stirring frequently, for 10-15 minutes or until potatoes are just tender.

2 Add tomatoes and cook for 5 minutes longer or until tomatoes are soft and pulpy. Stir in peas, 180 ml (6 fl oz) reserved cooking water, mango powder, turmeric, ground cumin and ground coriander and mix well to combine. Cook over a low heat for 5 minutes longer. Just prior to serving, stir in fresh coriander.

GUJARATI-STYLE BEANS

REALLY EASY!

Green beans quickly cooked with ginger, chillies and spices, then topped with fried black mustard seeds, coconut, fresh coriander and lemon juice.

Serves 6
3 tablespoons vegetable oil
3 teaspoons finely chopped fresh ginger
1-2 fresh red or green chillies, finely chopped
salt
500g (1 lb) green beans, chopped
125 ml (4 fl oz) water
1 teaspoon ground coriander
1 teaspoon ground cumin
1 teaspoon mango powder
1 teaspoon caster sugar
¼ teaspoon ground turmeric
½ teaspoon black mustard seeds
30g (1 oz) grated fresh or desiccated coconut
2-3 tablespoons chopped fresh coriander
1 tablespoon lemon juice

1 Heat 2 tablespoons oil in a heavy-based saucepan over a medium heat. Add ginger, chillies and salt to taste and allow to sizzle for 1 minute. Add beans and water, stir well to combine, then reduce heat and cook for 10 minutes.

2 Stir in ground coriander, cumin, mango powder, sugar and turmeric and cook, stirring occasionally, for 4-5 minutes or until beans are tender. Transfer beans to a serving dish.

3 Heat remaining oil in a metal ladle or very small pan and add black mustard seeds. When they start to sizzle and pop, pour over the beans. Sprinkle beans with coconut, fresh coriander and lemon juice.

SPICY MUSHROOMS

REALLY EASY!

Whole button mushrooms cooked in butter with spices and fresh coriander.

Serves 4

¼ teaspoon ground cumin
¼ teaspoon ground coriander
¼ teaspoon mango powder
¼ teaspoon caster sugar
¼ teaspoon paprika
¼ teaspoon ground turmeric
pinch black salt
30g (1 oz) butter
250g (8 oz) button mushrooms
2 tablespoons chopped fresh coriander
salt

1 Place cumin, ground coriander, mango powder, sugar, paprika, turmeric and black salt in a bowl and mix to combine.

2 Melt butter in a large frying pan, add mushrooms and cook for 5-7 minutes. Remove pan from heat and stir in spice mixture, fresh coriander and salt to taste.

GUJARATI-STYLE BEANS • SPICY MUSHROOMS

113

DHALS

Otherwise known as lentils and pulses, dhals are varieties of dried beans and peas, and they are eaten daily in some form or other in most Indian homes. In India there are very many ways of cooking dhal, each region having its own speciality. Sometimes it may be the consistency of soup and is poured over rice, at other times it may be very thick and spicy and mixed with vegetables and served with Indian bread. Unless you buy dhals specially cleaned and packed from large supermarkets, you must be diligent in picking over the dhal to remove any stalks, sticks, stones or discoloured beans. Then they must be washed thoroughly several times in cold water to remove all the dust. The long slow cooking necessary for most pulses means that the flavour of the vegetables and spices loose their intensity, so often a spice mixture is added at the end or for the last few minutes of cooking.

INDIAN DHAL

REALLY EASY!

Cooked lentils with added onion, spices and fiery cayenne pepper.

Serves 6
250g (8 oz) brown or red lentils
1 litre (1¾ pints) water
1 teaspoon ground turmeric
1 clove garlic, crushed
30g (1 oz) ghee or clarified butter
1 large onion, chopped
1 teaspoon garam masala
½ teaspoon ground ginger
1 teaspoon ground coriander
½ teaspoon cayenne pepper

1 Wash lentils in cold water.

2 Place lentils, water, turmeric and garlic in a large saucepan and bring to the boil. Cover and simmer, stirring occasionally, for 30 minutes or until lentils are cooked. Remove cover from pan, bring to the boil and boil to reduce excess liquid.

3 Melt ghee or butter in a large frying pan, add onion and cook for 5 minutes or until onion is soft. Stir in garam masala, ginger, coriander, and cayenne pepper and cook for 1 minute. Stir spice mixture into lentils and serve immediately.

MIXED LENTILS

EASY!

**A mixture of lentils, cooked and puréed and then
heated with a mixture of chillies, spices,
asafoetida (hing) and tamarind.
The unspiced lentil mixture freezes well. Simply
follow the recipe to the end of step 2, allow to
cool and freeze. When required, defrost and
complete the recipe as described.**

Serves 4

60g (2 oz) mung dhal (small yellow lentils)
60g (2 oz) channa dhal (yellow split peas)
60g (2 oz) thoor dhal (medium flat yellow lentils)
60g (2 oz) masoor dhal (pink lentils)
500 ml (16 fl oz) water
salt
2 tablespoons vegetable oil
¼ teaspoon ground turmeric
2 fresh red or green chillies, finely chopped
2 teaspoons finely chopped fresh ginger
½ teaspoon coriander seeds
1 teaspoon black mustard seeds
1 teaspoon fenugreek seeds
1 teaspoon yellow mustard seeds
1 teaspoon cumin seeds
2 branches fresh curry leaves or 12-16 dried curry leaves
750 ml (1 ¼ pints) hot water
¼ teaspoon asafoetida, (hing)
2 tablespoons concentrated tamarind
or 1 tablespoon tomato purée

1 Pick lentils over and remove any small sticks or stones,
then place lentils in a large bowl. Fill bowl with water
and, using your hands, stir until water is cloudy. Drain
and repeat until water is clear. You will probably need to

repeat the procedure 3-4 times. Drain, pour over fresh water and set lentils aside to soak for 45 minutes.

2 Drain lentils and place in a saucepan with 500 ml (16 fl oz) of water, salt to taste, 1 tablespoon oil and turmeric and bring to the boil over a medium heat, reduce heat and simmer, partially covered, for 15 minutes or until lentils are soft. Place lentil mixture in a food processor or blender and process until smooth. Set aside.

3 Heat remaining oil in a large saucepan, add chillies, ginger, coriander seeds, mustard seeds, fenugreek seeds, yellow mustard seeds, cumin seeds and curry leaves and cook, stirring, for 1 minute. Add puréed lentil mixture and cook, stirring, for 2 minutes longer. Stir in 750 ml (1¼ pints) hot water and bring to the boil. Add asafoetida and tamarind or tomato purée and cook for 2-5 minutes longer or until pulpy.

RED LENTILS AND TOMATO AND ONION SAUCE

EASY!

Lentils boiled in water with spices until soft and then mixed with a tomato, onion and chilli sauce. A separate mixture of spices is added at the end of cooking for extra flavour.

Serves 4-6
500 ml (16 fl oz) water
300g (10 oz) red lentils, cleaned and soaked
1 teaspoon vegetable oil
1 teaspoon finely chopped fresh ginger
¼ teaspoon ground turmeric
salt

Tomato And Onion Sauce
2 tablespoons vegetable oil
2 teaspoons finely chopped fresh ginger
2 fresh red or green chillies, chopped
3 onions, minced or finely chopped
4 tomatoes, skinned and diced
600 ml (1 pint) water
30g (1 oz) ghee or butter
¼ teaspoon cumin seeds
¼ teaspoon fennel seeds
¼ teaspoon black mustard seeds
¼ teaspoon fenugreek seeds
¼ teaspoon black onion seeds
3 dried red chillies
2 bay leaves
2 teaspoons garlic paste (optional)

1 Place 500 ml (16 fl oz) water in a saucepan and bring to the boil. Add lentils, 1 teaspoon oil, ginger, turmeric and salt to taste and cook, partially covered, for 15-20 minutes or until lentils are soft and pulpy.

2 To make sauce, heat oil in a heavy-based saucepan, add ginger, chillies and onions, cover and cook over a medium heat for 10-15 minutes or until onions are golden. Stir in tomatoes and cook over a low heat for 10-15 minutes or until tomatoes are soft. Stir lentil mixture and 600 ml (1 pint) water into tomato mixture and bring to the boil.

3 Heat ghee or butter in a frying pan, add cumin seeds, fennel seeds, mustard seeds, fenugreek seeds, black onion seeds, chillies, bay leaves and garlic paste (if using) and cook for 2 minutes. Stir spice mixture into boiling lentil mixture, cover and cook for 2 minutes longer.

RED LENTILS AND TOMATO AND ONION SAUCE

BOMBAY HOT LENTILS

E A S Y !

**A hot and spicy mixture of cooked, mashed
lentils with the added sharpness of tamarind.**

Serves 4
500 ml (16 fl oz) water
*200g (7 oz) mung dhal (small yellow lentils), cleaned
and soaked*
½ teaspoon ground turmeric
1 teaspoon finely chopped fresh ginger
1 tablespoon vegetable oil
salt
1 tablespoon tamarind
250 ml (8 fl oz) hot water
1 litre (1 ¾ pints) water
1 tablespoon brown sugar
2 tablespoons fresh chopped coriander
3 tablespoons grated coconut
2 teaspoons garam masala

Whole Spice Mixture
90g (3 oz) ghee or butter
1 teaspoon cumin seeds
1 teaspoon black mustard seeds
¼ teaspoon fenugreek seeds
2 tablespoons chopped curry leaves
3 fresh red or green chillies, finely chopped
2 teaspoons finely chopped fresh ginger
salt

1 Place 500 ml (16 fl oz) water in a large saucepan and
bring to the boil. Stir in lentils, turmeric, ginger, oil and
salt to taste and cook over a low heat, stirring occasionally, for 30-45 minutes or until lentils are very soft.
Remove pan from heat and mash lentil mixture.

2 Place tamarind in a small bowl, pour over 250 ml (8 fl oz) hot water and set aside to soak for 20 minutes. Drain liquid from tamarind mixture, then push tamarind pulp through a fine sieve and set aside.

3 For spice mixture, heat ghee or butter in a separate large saucepan, add cumin seeds, mustard seeds, fenugreek seeds, curry leaves, chillies, ginger and salt to taste and cook, stirring, for 1 minute. Add lentil mixture and 1 litre (1¾ pints) water to spice mixture and bring to the boil. Stir reserved tamarind pulp and brown sugar into lentil mixture and cook, stirring occasionally, for 5 minutes longer.

4 Stir in fresh coriander, coconut and garam masala and cook for 2 minutes longer.

BOMBAY HOT LENTILS

LENTILS WITH POORI

EASY!

A firm mixture of cooked lentils, pressed into a mould and then turned out onto a dish and garnished with cooked onions, spices and fresh coriander.

Serves 6

750 ml (1¼ pints) water
400g (14 oz) mung dhal (small yellow lentils), cleaned
salt
2 teaspoons finely chopped fresh ginger
2 tablespoons vegetable oil
½ teaspoon ground turmeric
2 onions, thinly sliced
¼ teaspoon paprika
¼ teaspoon mango powder
¼ teaspoon ground cumin
2 tablespoons chopped fresh coriander
16 Pooris, or other Indian bread

1 Place water in a large saucepan, add lentils, salt to taste, ginger, 1 tablespoon oil and turmeric and cook, partially covered, over a medium heat for 30 minutes. Beat with a hand beater, then reduce heat to the lowest possible setting and simmer for 10 minutes, until mixture is fairly dry. Stir to prevent sticking.

2 Heat remaining oil in a small frying pan, add onions and cook, stirring frequently, for 5 minutes or until onions are soft and golden.

3 Combine paprika, mango powder and cumin. To serve, press lentil mixture into a lightly oiled mould, then turn onto a serving plate. Surround with the onions and sprinkle with spice mixture and fresh coriander. Serve with Pooris.

VEGETABLE AND LENTIL CURRY

REALLY EASY!

Lentils cooked with tomatoes to which are added spices and chunks of pumpkin, carrots and cauliflower, sliced onion and whole almonds. Topped with yogurt to serve.

Serves 4

1 tablespoon olive oil
1 onion, sliced
1 clove garlic, crushed
1 teaspoon ground cumin
1 teaspoon ground coriander
1 teaspoon ground turmeric
2 carrots, sliced
125g (4 oz) red lentils
400g (14 oz) canned tomatoes, undrained and mashed
375 ml (12 fl oz) vegetable stock or water
1 teaspoon chilli sauce , or according to taste
500g (1 lb) pumpkin or potatoes, cut into 2 cm (¾ inch) cubes
½ cauliflower, cut into florets
60g (2 oz) blanched almonds
freshly ground black pepper
4 tablespoons natural yogurt

1 Heat oil in a large saucepan, add onion, garlic, cumin, coriander, turmeric and carrots and cook for 5 minutes or until onion is soft.

2 Stir in lentils, tomatoes and stock or water and bring to the boil. Reduce heat, cover and simmer for 15 minutes.

3 Add chilli sauce, pumpkin (or potato) and cauliflower and cook for 15-20 minutes longer or until pumpkin (or potato) is tender. Stir in almonds and black pepper to taste. Serve in bowls and top with yogurt.

LENTILS WITH POORI • VEGETABLE AND LENTIL CURRY

SPICY CHICKPEAS WITH ONIONS AND TOMATOES

EASY!

Onions, spices, a few cooked chickpeas and tomatoes are made into a purée, to which are added the remaining whole cooked chickpeas and extra spices. An excellent addition to a vegetarian meal, this dish is ideally served with Bhutoras (see p 142).

Serves 4

400g (14 oz) dried chickpeas
¼ teaspoon bicarbonate of soda
salt
water
2 onions, roughly chopped
2 teaspoons finely chopped fresh ginger
2 fresh red or green chillies, finely chopped
2-3 cloves garlic, finely chopped
1 tablespoon vegetable oil
2 bay leaves
2 teaspoons whole cumin seeds
5 tomatoes, chopped
pinch garam masala
½ teaspoon ground coriander
½ teaspoon ground cumin
pinch mango powder
pinch ground fennel
pinch ground mace or nutmeg
pinch ground fenugreek
½ teaspoon ground turmeric

1 Place chickpeas, bicarbonate of soda and 1 teaspoon salt in a large bowl. Pour over enough water to cover. Cover and set aside to soak overnight.

2 Drain chickpeas and place in a saucepan. Cover with clean water, bring to the boil and boil for 10 minutes. Reduce heat and simmer for 1 hour or until chickpeas are tender. Drain and reserve cooking liquid.

3 Place 6 tablespoons cooked chickpeas, onions, ginger, chillies and garlic in a food processor or blender and process until smooth. Heat oil in a heavy-based frying pan, add onion mixture, bay leaves, cumin seeds and salt to taste and cook over a very low heat, stirring frequently, for 30-40 minutes or until golden.

4 Stir in tomatoes and cook for 10-15 minutes longer or until tomatoes are soft and pulpy. Add remaining chickpeas, bring to the boil over a low heat, adding a little of reserved cooking liquid if mixture seems dry.

5 Combine garam masala, coriander, cumin, mango powder, fennel, mace or nutmeg, fenugreek and turmeric. Stir spice mixture into chickpea mixture and simmer for 5 minutes.

125

LENTIL AND RICE DUMPLINGS

Little dumplings made with urad dhal flour, ground rice, spices, nuts, herbs and sultanas. The dumplings are deep fried and then soaked in warm water and squeezed dry and served with a covering of natural yogurt topped with spices.

Serves 4-6

180g (6 oz) white urad dhal flour
90g (3 oz) ground rice (fine rice flour)
4 fresh green chillies, finely chopped
1 teaspoon finely chopped fresh ginger
¼ teaspoon bicarbonate of soda
2 teaspoons roughly chopped sultanas
2 teaspoons chopped salted cashews
2 teaspoons chopped blanched almonds
salt
3-4 tablespoons chopped fresh coriander
water
vegetable oil for deep-frying
170g (6 oz) natural yogurt
¼ teaspoon mango powder
¼ teaspoon ground cumin
¼ teaspoon ground coriander
¼ teaspoon paprika
¼ teaspoon black salt
1 tablespoon black mustard seeds
5-7 fresh or dried curry leaves

1 Place dhal flour, ground rice, chillies, ginger, bicarbonate of soda, sultanas, cashews, almonds, salt to taste and half the fresh coriander in a bowl. Stir in enough water to make a stiff, smooth batter, mix well to combine, cover and set aside to stand for 1 hour.

2 Heat oil in a wok, until a cube of bread, dropped in,

browns in 50 seconds. Scoop a spoonful of batter into the palm of your hand and gently pat to form a dumpling. Cook 4-5 dumplings at a time in hot oil until golden.

3 Using a slotted spoon, remove dumplings from oil and drop into a bowl of warm water. Allow dumplings to soak for 5-7 minutes, then remove and squeeze between the palms of your hands to flatten and remove excess water. Arrange dumplings on a flat serving dish.

4 Place yogurt and 60 ml (2 fl oz) water in a bowl and beat until smooth. Spoon a little yogurt mixture over each dumpling to completely cover.

5 Combine mango powder, cumin, ground coriander, paprika and black salt and set aside. Remove 2 tablespoons of hot oil from wok, place in a metal ladle, or very small saucepan, and heat over a low heat. Add black mustard seeds and curry leaves and continue to heat until they sizzle. Pour oil mixture evenly over dumplings, then sprinkle with spice mixture and remaining fresh coriander. Serve immediately.

RICE

The best type of rice to buy for Indian dishes is
long-grain, and one that is especially good is
basmati which has long slender grains. Basmati
is grown in the foothills of the Himalayas and it is
aged before it is sold, giving it a special aroma
and nutty flavour. It is not advisable to buy quick-
cooking or instant rice or even a partially cooked
variety, as these tend to overcook and give a
mushy result. Washing the rice grains before
cooking rinses off any excess starch and helps
the rice to remain separate when cooked.

PLAIN WHITE RICE

REALLY EASY!

To make a yellow coloured, slightly aromatic rice, add a little ground turmeric to the rice and water before cooking.

Serves 6
1 litre (1¾ pints) water
400g (14 oz) basmati rice, washed
1 teaspoon lemon juice
1 teaspoon vegetable oil
salt

1 Place water in a large heavy-based saucepan and bring to the boil. Stir in rice, lemon juice, oil and salt to taste, cover and simmer for 15 minutes or until rice is cooked.

To microwave: Place rice, lemon juice and oil in a large microwave-safe container, pour over boiling water, cover and cook on HIGH (100%) for 8 minutes, then on LOW (30%) for 10-12 minutes longer or until liquid is absorbed and rice is tender.

PLAIN WHITE RICE

SPICY RICE

E A S Y !

Boiled rice cooked with the addition of a muslin bag filled with spices which gives the rice a subtle flavour. Make sure that the spice bag is very securely tied because if anything spills out the rice will have a bitter taste.

Serves 6
1.2 litres (2 pints) water
400g (14 oz) long-grain rice
1 teaspoon lemon juice
salt

Spice Bag
¼ teaspoon black peppercorns
¼ teaspoon black onion seeds
¼ teaspoon cumin seeds
2 dried red chillies
1 cinnamon stick, broken in half
2 black cardamom pods
2 teaspoons finely chopped fresh ginger
2 bay leaves
1 piece muslin, 12-15 cm (5-6 inch) square

1 To make Spice Bag, place peppercorns, black onion seeds, cumin seeds, chillies, cinnamon, cardamom pods, ginger and bay leaves in the centre of the piece of muslin. Draw up corners and tie securely.

2 Place water in a large saucepan and bring to the boil. Stir in rice, lemon juice and salt to taste. Add Spice Bag and bring back to the boil, then reduce heat to low, cover and simmer for 12-15 minutes or until rice is cooked. Remove Spice Bag before serving.

To microwave: Place water, rice, lemon juice, salt to taste and Spice Bag in a large microwave-safe container, cover and cook on HIGH (100%) for 8-10 minutes, then cook on MEDIUM (70%) for 10 minutes longer. Remove Spice Bag before serving.

FRESH HERB PULLAO

REALLY EASY!

This is a pilau, or pilaf, made with rice, water, spices and lots of fresh herbs, which are all simmered gently together until the water is absorbed and the rice is tender.

Serves 8

2 tablespoons vegetable oil
1 teaspoon cumin seeds
1 teaspoon black mustard seeds
½ teaspoon fennel seeds
¼ teaspoon fenugreek seeds
1 stick cinnamon
2 cardamom pods, lightly crushed
2 bay leaves
1 fresh red or green chilli, finely chopped
2 teaspoons finely chopped fresh ginger
salt
400g (14 oz) basmati rice
1 tablespoon lemon juice
2 tablespoons chopped fresh coriander
2 tablespoons chopped fresh dill
1 tablespoon chopped fresh mint
1 tablespoon chopped fresh basil
1 tablespoon snipped fresh chives
1 litre (1¾ pints) water

1 Heat oil in a heavy-based saucepan. Add cumin seeds, mustard seeds, fennel seeds, fenugreek seeds, cinnamon stick, cardamom pods, bay leaves, chilli, ginger and salt to taste and cook, stirring, for 2 minutes. Stir in rice, lemon juice, coriander, dill, mint, basil, chives and water and bring to the boil. Reduce heat to low, cover and simmer for 15-20 minutes or until cooked. Remove bay leaves and cinnamon stick before serving.

RICE WITH PEAS AND SPICES

REALLY EASY!

Rice cooked with the addition of chilli, spices, fresh herbs, peas and saffron to give a golden colour.

Serves 6
2 tablespoons vegetable oil
2 teaspoons finely chopped fresh ginger
1 fresh red or green chilli, finely chopped
¼ teaspoon cumin seeds
¼ teaspoon black mustard seeds
3-4 fresh or dried curry leaves
salt
1 tablespoon chopped fresh basil
1 tablespoon chopped fresh mint
1 tablespoon chopped fresh coriander
90g (3 oz) fresh or frozen peas, half-cooked
400g (14 oz) long-grain rice
1 litre (1¾ pints) boiling water
10-12 strands saffron soaked in a little warm water
(optional)

1 Heat oil in a large heavy-based saucepan, add ginger, chilli, cumin seeds, mustard seeds, curry leaves and salt to taste and cook, stirring, for 1 minute.

2 Stir in basil, mint, coriander, peas, rice, water and saffron mixture (if using), cover and bring to the boil. Reduce heat to low and cook for 15 minutes or until rice is cooked.

ROSE-SCENTED SAFFRON RICE

EASY!

**A fragrant dish of rice, minced lamb, mixed
spice, currants, almonds, rosewater and saffron.
Saffron not only colours the rice, but also
gives it a delicious fragrance. Such fragrant
and coloured rice dishes are often made for
special occasions in India.**

Serves 6

*500g (1 lb) basmati rice, washed
60g (2 oz) ghee or butter
1 onion, chopped
250g (8 oz) minced lean lamb
½ teaspoon mixed spice
60g (2 oz) currants
½ teaspoon powdered saffron
2 tablespoons rosewater
1 litre (1¾ pints) chicken stock
60g (2 oz) blanched almonds, toasted*

1 Place rice in a large bowl, cover with cold water and
set aside to stand for 30 minutes.

2 Heat ghee or butter in a large heavy-based frying pan
over a medium heat, add the onion and cook for 5
minutes or until soft. Increase heat, add lamb and cook
until browned. Stir in mixed spice and currants and cook
for 1 minute longer. Remove pan from heat, set aside
and keep warm.

3 Place saffron and rosewater in a cup and mix to
combine. Place chicken stock and 2 teaspoons rosewater
mixture in a large saucepan and bring to the boil. Drain
rice, add to stock mixture and bring back to the boil,
stirring occasionally. Reduce heat, cover and simmer for
30 minutes.

4 Mix meat mixture into rice, remove pan from heat, cover and set aside to stand for 5 minutes before serving. To serve, sprinkle with remaining rosewater mixture and top with almonds.

SPICED CAULIFLOWER AND CUMIN PILAU

REALLY EASY!

This is a quick dish of cauliflower cooked with onion, cumin and spices to which is added cooked rice, cashew nuts and sultanas.

Serves 4
60g (2 oz) butter
1 onion, chopped
1 clove garlic, crushed
1 tablespoon cumin seeds
1 cinnamon stick
2 bay leaves
1 teaspoon ground cardamom
1 medium cauliflower, broken into small florets
90 ml (3 fl oz) water
300g (10 oz) basmati rice, cooked
125g (4 oz) roasted cashew nuts
60g (2 oz) sultanas

1 Melt butter in a large frying pan, add onion and cook for 4-5 minutes or until onion is soft. Stir in garlic, cumin seeds, cinnamon, bay leaves and cardamom and cook for 1 minute.

2 Add cauliflower and water, cover and cook for 5 minutes or until cauliflower is tender.

3 Stir in rice, cashew nuts and sultanas and cook for 5 minutes longer or until heated through. Remove bay leaves and cinnamon stick before serving.

BREADS

Most Indian breads are unleavened flat breads
which are not only the basic dietary staple, but
are also used to hold or scoop up food, so
replacing plates, knives and forks. They are very
easy to make and are simply rolled or patted into
shape. In India, a slightly concave heavy iron
cooking pan called a 'tava' is used for top of the
stove breads, but you can use a heavy based
griddle or frying pan equally well. When ovens
are used they are often made of clay or bricks
and may be built in pits, and breads such as
Naan are just slapped onto the hot wall or floor
of the oven to cook. You can use a very hot
conventional oven, but make sure you have good
heavy duty baking trays that will not buckle. To
enjoy Indian breads at their best, they should be
made just before a meal and eaten hot within a
few minutes of cooking.

CHAPATIS

EASY!

These are round, flat unleavened breads made from sieved wholemeal flour. They are quickly cooked in a large frying pan or on a griddle.

Makes 12
300g (10 oz) wholemeal flour
60g (2 oz) plain flour
salt
vegetable oil, for dough and frying
250 ml (8 fl oz) lukewarm water

1 Sift wholemeal flour, 30g (1 oz) plain flour and salt to taste, into a large bowl. Discard husks. Mix in 1 tablespoon oil and enough water to form a firm dough. Turn dough onto a lightly floured surface and knead for 10 minutes or until dough is smooth. Place dough in a bowl, cover and set aside for 1 hour.

2 Knead dough again then divide into 12 equal portions. Roll each portion into a ball. Flatten each ball, sprinkle with a little of the remaining flour and roll out until quite thin to make an oval shape. Rub a little oil onto each oval.

3 Place thumb and middle finger on each side of every oval and squeeze together to form 2 circles. Fold circles together so oiled sides are in the centre, dust with a little more flour and roll out again.

4 Heat a little oil in a frying pan over a medium heat and cook Chapatis one at a time for 2-3 minutes each side, pressing down lightly if they puff up. Drain on absorbent kitchen paper.

POORIS

EASY!

These are similar to Chapatis, but are smaller and puffed up like little cushions because they are deep fried. When cooking Pooris the temperature of the oil is very important, not hot enough and the Pooris will not rise, too hot and the Pooris will burn and again not rise. Test the temperature first with a small piece of dough.

Makes 16
300g (12 oz) wholemeal flour
125g (4 oz) plain flour
salt
250 ml (8 fl oz) water
vegetable oil for dough and deep-frying

1 Sift wholemeal flour, flour and salt to taste, into a bowl. Discard husks. Stir in 1 teaspoon oil and enough water to form a soft dough. Turn dough onto a lightly floured surface and knead until smooth. Place dough in a bowl, cover and set aside for 30 minutes.

2 Knead dough again for 5 minutes and divide into 16 equal portions. Roll each portion into a ball. Flatten each ball and roll out to form a thin 10 cm (4 inch) round.

3 Heat oil in a wok or deep pan until very hot, but not smoking (190°C ,375°F). Slip 1 poori into oil at an angle so that poori is submerged in oil. Using a large flat round slotted spoon gently hold Poori under oil for 2-3 seconds or until you feel it rise. Rapidly spoon oil over Poori and as soon as it puffs up and blisters, turn it over and continue spooning oil over for 3-4 seconds longer. Remove and drain on absorbent kitchen paper.

NAAN

EASY!

A leavened bread made with white flour and yogurt. It is the yogurt that ferments the dough and adds flavour. Traditionally these breads are baked in a clay oven sunk into the ground but they can be sucessfully cooked in a hot oven or under the grill.

Makes 4

500g (1 lb) self-raising flour
4 tablespoons plain live yogurt
1 teaspoon salt
about 125 ml (4 fl oz) lukewarm water

1 Put the flour, yogurt and salt into a bowl. Add the water, a little at a time, to make a soft, slightly sticky dough. Knead lightly and then cover with a damp tea-towel and leave in a warm place for about 1 hour.

2 Preheat the oven to 220C,425F,Gas 7 or preheat the grill to high. With lightly floured hands pull dough into four pieces. Roll out into 18 cm (7 inch) circles. To make into the traditional tear drop shape, stretch one side a little.

3 Place on greased baking trays in the preheated oven for about 10 minutes until puffy and brown. Alternatively, cook under a hot grill until puffed up and speckled brown. Serve warm.

VARIATIONS:

Spiced Naan – Add to the flour, 1 teaspoon finely chopped fresh coriander, ½ teaspoon black onion seeds, ½ teaspoon sesame seeds, ¼ teaspoon cumin seeds and ¼ teaspoon fennel seeds. Complete recipe as above.

Keema Naan – Cook 1 tablespoon finely chopped onion and 125g (4 oz) minced lamb in a pan with a little oil for about 5 minutes. Add ¼ teaspoon ground cumin and cook for a further 2-3 minutes. Allow to become completely cold. Roll dough out into rounds as in recipe and place a little of the lamb mixture in the centre of each round. bring the sides of the dough to the centre to cover the meat and then turn over and roll out to a flat round and complete recipe as above.

Peshwari Naan – Mix together 90g (3 oz) ground almonds, 1 tablespoon desiccated coconut, 1 tablespoon caster sugar, 1 tablespoon chopped sultanas and 15g (½ oz) softened butter. Roll the dough out into rounds and proceed as for Keema Naan.

BHUTORAS

EASY!

These are made from leavened dough with the added richness of melted ghee. They are deep-fried until puffed up and golden.

Makes 16
3 teaspoons sugar
150g (5 oz) plain flour
¾ teaspoon bicarbonate of soda
170g (6 oz) plain live yogurt
470g (15 oz) sifted wholemeal flour
salt
1½ tablespoons melted ghee or butter
180 ml (6 fl oz) lukewarm water
vegetable oil for deep-frying

1 Place sugar, flour, bicarbonate of soda and yogurt in a bowl and mix to combine. Cover with plastic food wrap and set aside to ferment overnight.

2 About 3 hours before you intend to cook Bhutoras, place wholemeal flour, salt to taste, ghee or butter and water in a bowl. Stir in yogurt mixture and mix to form a dough. Turn dough onto a lightly floured surface and knead well for 15 minutes, adding flour if necessary, to make a firm smooth dough.

3 Divide dough into 16 equal portions and roll out each portion to form a thin round. Heat oil in a wok until very hot but not smoking (190°C, 375°F). Slip one Bhutora into oil at an angle so that it is submerged in oil. Using a large flat round slotted spoon gently hold Bhutora under oil for 2-3 seconds or until you feel it rise. Rapidly spoon oil over Bhutora and as soon as it puffs up and blisters, turn it over and continue spooning oil over until Bhutora puffs and blisters again. Remove and drain on absorbent kitchen paper.

SPICY WHOLEMEAL PARATHAS

EASY!

**Parathas are flat unleavened breads and in
this version they have a filling of cumin,
potato and cheese.**

Makes 12

350g (12 oz) plain flour
150g (5 oz) wholemeal flour
125g (4 oz) butter
375 ml (12 fl oz) water
250g (8 oz) mashed potato
125g (4 oz) grated mature Cheddar cheese
2 teaspoons curry powder
1 teaspoon ground cumin
vegetable oil for frying

1 Place the flour and wholemeal flour in a bowl and mix well together. Add 60g (2 oz) butter and rub into the flour until the mixture resembles coarse breadcrumbs.

2 Add enough water to mix to a stiff but not sticky dough. Turn dough onto a lightly floured surface and knead for 5 minutes or until smooth. Set aside to stand for 5 minutes.

3 Place mashed potato, cheese, curry powder and cumin in a bowl and mix to combine.

4 Divide dough into twelve equal portions and press out each portion to form a 10 cm (4 inch) circle. Divide potato mixture between dough circles and spread evenly over the dough, leaving a border around the edge. Fold dough circles in half to enclose the filling, then carefully roll again to form a 10 cm (4 inch) circle.

5 Melt remaining butter and a little vegetable oil in a large frying pan and cook a few parathas at a time for 3-4 minutes each side or until golden and cooked through.

CHUTNEYS AND RAITHAS

Chutneys play a very important part in an Indian meal and are often served with snacks before a meal as well as with the main dishes themselves. Chutneys can be sweet, sour, mild or hot and there are no do's and don'ts about which ones you serve with a particular dish, it's entirely up to your own preference. Most chutneys should be kept in the fridge and relatively small quantities are made as they are best eaten fresh.

Raithas are yogurt-based acompaniments. They are very simple to make from natural yogurt and the addition of a vegetable, fruit or herb. They are cool and refreshing and excellent with very hot or spicy curries.

MINT AND TOMATO CHUTNEY

REALLY EASY!

A tomato chutney well flavoured with mint, ginger and chillies. This chutney should be kept in the fridge and will last about 4-6 weeks.

Makes 1 x 125g (4 oz) jar
4 large tomatoes, diced
4 tablespoons chopped fresh mint
90g (3 oz) brown sugar
1 cinnamon stick
2 bay leaves
1 teaspoon mixed spice
2 teaspoons finely chopped fresh ginger
2 fresh red or green chillies, chopped
60 ml (2 fl oz) white wine vinegar

1 Place tomatoes, mint, sugar, cinnamon stick, bay leaves, mixed spice, ginger, chillies and vinegar in a heavy-based saucepan and cook over a low heat, stirring every 5 minutes, for 45 minutes or until mixture reduces and thickens. Remove cinnamon stick and bay leaves.

2 Spoon chutney into a warm sterilised jar, cover and label when cold.

RED CHILLI CHUTNEY

REALLY EASY!

**A very hot mixture of chillies and garlic puréed
with a little water to make a paste.
When handling fresh chillies, do not put your
hands near your eyes or allow them to touch your
lips. To avoid discomfort and burning, you might
like to wear rubber gloves.**

Makes 1 x 125g (4 oz) jar
10-12 fresh red chillies
10-12 cloves garlic
pinch caster sugar (optional)
salt
water

1 Place chillies, garlic, sugar (if using) and salt to taste in
a food processor or blender and process to chop. With
machine running, add enough water to form a paste.
Store in the refrigerator in an airtight container.

CORIANDER AND MINT CHUTNEY

REALLY EASY!

A purée of fresh coriander and mint, flavoured with chillies, ginger, garlic and lemon.

Makes 1 x 250g (8 oz) jar

3 bunches fresh coriander, leaves removed
1 bunch fresh mint, leaves removed
6-8 fresh green chillies
3 teaspoons finely chopped fresh ginger
6 cloves garlic, finely chopped
2 tablespoons lemon juice
1 tablespoon caster sugar
60 ml (2 fl oz) water
salt

1 Place coriander leaves, mint leaves, chillies, ginger, garlic, lemon juice, sugar, water and salt to taste in a food processor or blender and process to a paste.

2 Spoon chutney into a sterilised jar, cover and refrigerate until ready to use.

MANGO CHUTNEY

REALLY EASY!

One of the best known Indian chutneys, this recipe combines mangos, raisins, spices, sugar and vinegar to make a mellow, fruity mixture. For sweeter chutney use the larger quantity of sugar and for a less sweet chutney use the smaller quantity. The chutney should be stored in the fridge.

Makes 1 x 250g (8 oz) jar

250g (8 oz) raisins
2 x 400g (14 oz) canned mangos, drained and cut into cubes, or 4 ripe mangos, peeled and cut into cubes
1½ tablespoons finely chopped fresh ginger
2 cloves garlic, finely chopped
3 teaspoons paprika
1 cinnamon stick
4 cloves
2 bay leaves
½ teaspoon mixed spice
3 tablespoons sultanas
60 ml (2 fl oz) cider vinegar
170-250g (5½-8 oz) brown sugar

1 Place raisins in a small bowl, cover with warm water and set aside to soak for 30 minutes. Drain.

2 Place mangos, ginger, garlic, paprika, cinnamon stick, cloves, bay leaves, mixed spice, sultanas, vinegar, sugar and raisins in a large heavy-based saucepan. Cover and cook over a low heat, stirring occasionally, for 1 hour or until chutney is thick. Remove bay leaves and cinnamon stick before serving.

3 Spoon chutney into a warm sterilised jar. Cover and label when cold. Store in the refrigerator.

SESAME SEED CHUTNEY

EASY!

**Toasted sesame seeds mixed with fresh
coriander and mint and then puréed with the
sharp acidic tamarind concentrate and water.**

Makes 1 x 125g (4 oz) jar

75g (2½ oz) sesame seeds
1 bunch fresh coriander, leaves removed
1 bunch fresh mint, leaves removed
5 fresh green chillies
60 ml (2 fl oz) tamarind concentrate
6-7 tablespoons water
½ teaspoon salt

1 Place sesame seeds in a cast-iron frying pan and dry-fry over a low heat until dark brown in colour. Place sesame seeds in a food processor or blender and process to grind. Add coriander, mint, chillies, tamarind concentrate, water and salt and process to make a smooth paste. Alternatively use a pestle and mortar to make the paste. Spoon chutney into a sterilised jar, cover and label. Store in the refrigerator.

FRUIT CHUTNEY

REALLY EASY!

Dried chopped peaches and apricots with apples and sultanas, cooked with sugar and vinegar until soft and pulpy.

Makes 2 x 250g (8 oz) jars

125g (4 oz) dried peaches, chopped
125g (4 oz) dried apricots, chopped
500g (1 lb) Granny Smith apples, cored, peeled and chopped
2 teaspoons finely chopped fresh ginger
125g (4 oz) sultanas
500 ml (16 fl oz) white vinegar
2 teaspoons salt
400g (14 oz) caster sugar
5 cloves garlic, finely chopped
¾ teaspoon cayenne pepper (optional)

1 Place peaches, apricots, apples, ginger, sultanas, vinegar, salt, sugar, garlic and cayenne pepper (if using) in a large heavy-based saucepan. Cover and cook over a low heat, stirring occasionally, for 1½ hours or until mixture is soft and pulpy.

2 Spoon chutney into hot sterilised jars. When cold, cover and label. Store in the refrigerator.

PLAIN RAITHA

R E A L L Y   E A S Y !

Natural yogurt and yogurt-based dishes are refreshing accompaniments to spicy food.

Makes 250 ml (8 fl oz)
170g (6 oz) natural yogurt
60 ml (2 fl oz) water
salt
freshly ground black pepper

1 Place yogurt, water, and salt and black pepper to taste in a bowl and beat to combine.

SPINACH RAITHA

R E A L L Y   E A S Y !

Cooked and puréed spinach mixed with yogurt, spices and chillies

Makes 250 ml (8 fl oz)
500g (1 lb) young spinach
170g (6 oz) natural yogurt
pinch salt
pinch freshly ground black pepper
pinch paprika
pinch mango powder
2 small fresh red or green chillies, chopped

1 Steam or microwave spinach until soft. Drain, squeezing to remove excess liquid. Place spinach in a food processor or blender and process to make a purée.

2 Place yogurt in a bowl and beat until smooth. Stir in salt, black pepper, paprika, mango powder, chillies and spinach and mix to combine.

151

FRESH HERB RAITHA

REALLY EASY!

**Natural yogurt mixed with a selection of
freshly chopped herbs**

Makes 375 ml (12 fl oz)
170g (6 oz) natural yogurt
60 ml (2 fl oz) water
1 tablespoon chopped fresh coriander
*2-3 large sprigs fresh mint, leaves removed and coarsely
chopped*
*2-3 large sprigs fresh basil, leaves removed and coarsely
chopped*
2-3 large sprigs fresh dill, coarsely chopped
12 fresh chives, snipped
salt

1 Place yogurt and water in a bowl and whip until
smooth. Add coriander, mint, basil, dill, chives and salt to
taste and mix to combine.

APPLE RAITHA

REALLY EASY!

A cool mixture of natural yogurt, apple, spices and chopped fresh herbs.

Makes 375 ml (12 fl oz)
170g (6 oz) natural yogurt
3-4 tablespoons water
salt
1 green apple, cored, peeled and grated
¼ teaspoon ground cumin
¼ teaspoon ground coriander
¼ teaspoon paprika
¼ teaspoon mango powder
2 teaspoons chopped fresh coriander
2 teaspoons chopped fresh mint

1 Place yogurt, water and salt to taste in a bowl and beat until smooth. Add apple, cumin, ground coriander, paprika and mango powder and mix well. Spoon into a serving dish and sprinkle with fresh coriander and mint.

DESSERTS

Most Indian desserts are very rich, sweet, milk-based dishes. Due to the intense heat and lack of refrigeration, fresh milk cannot be stored in many parts of India, so a form of condensed milk is made by boiling fresh milk for 1–1½ hours until it is a half or a third of its original quantity. This can be kept without refrigeration and the milk puddings made with it ensure a supply of dairy produce in the diet. For speed you can use evaporated milk in recipes that call for boiled down milk. Favourite flavourings for desserts are cardamom, pistachio, almond and rosewater.

To end a hot spicy meal, you can just serve cooling slices of fresh fruits such as mango, melon, pineapple, apricots or whatever is in season. Several different fruits can be mixed together and lightly dressed with lime juice.

MANGO CREAM

REALLY EASY!

A fresh-tasting creamy dessert made with mangos, lemon juice and cream, the ideal end to a spicy meal.

Serves 4

2 ripe mangos or 400g (14 oz) canned mango flesh, chopped
2 tablespoons lemon juice
250 ml (8 fl oz) double cream
2 tablespoons icing sugar
mango slices to garnish

1 If using fresh mangoes, peel and cut flesh into large cubes. Place mango flesh and lemon juice in a food processor or blender and process until smooth.

2 Place cream and icing sugar in a mixing bowl and beat until soft peaks form. Fold mango purée into cream. Spoon into individual serving dishes. Decorate with a slice of mango and chill.

GULAB JAMAN

EASY!

Very sweet milk balls that are fried and then served in warm syrup.

Serves 6
350g (12 oz) granulated sugar
785 ml (1¼ pints) water
6 drops rosewater
180g (6 oz) low fat powdered milk
3 tablespoons self-raising flour
3 teaspoons semolina
3 tablespoons ghee
8 small cardamoms, shelled and seeds ground
milk to mix
vegetable oil for deep-frying

1 Put the sugar and water into a saucepan and heat gently until sugar has dissolved. Increase the heat and boil for 2-3 minutes to make a syrup. Stir in the rosewater and put to one side.

2 Put the powdered milk, flour, semolina, ghee and ground cardamom into a bowl. Add enough milk to mix to a soft dough. Shape into about 20 walnut-sized balls.

3 Heat the oil in a wok or deep pan and gently fry the balls, a few at a time. They should be cooked gently and will take 4-5 minutes to swell slightly and turn reddish brown in colour. Once cooked, drain well and add to the warm syrup. Serve at room temperature or slightly warm.

PISTACHIO AND ALMOND KULFI

REALLY EASY!

A traditional Indian ice cream made by boiling milk down to a third of its original quantity. Sugar and flavourings are then added and the mixture is frozen in small conical moulds. This recipe uses evaporated milk which cuts out the long process of boiling the milk.

Serves 6
2 x 400g (14oz) cans evaporated milk
4 green cardamom pods, split
90g (3 oz) caster sugar
90g (3 oz) shelled pistachios, skinned and ground or finely chopped
few drops almond essence
1 tablespoon chopped pistachios
1 tablespoon chopped almonds

1 Put evaporated milk, cardamom pods and sugar into a pan and heat gently until the sugar has dissolved. Remove from heat and allow to cool, stirring from time to time.

2 Strain the milk into a bowl. Stir in the ground pistachios and almond essence. Pour into a container and freeze for about 1½ hours or until half frozen. Remove and stir well until smooth. Put into small conical moulds or use dariole moulds or small yogurt pots. Cover and return to freezer and freeze overnight.

3 To serve, remove moulds from freezer and leave at room temperature for 5-10 minutes. Gently ease out onto serving plates. Sprinkle with chopped pistachios and almonds and serve.

GULAB JAMAN • PISTACHIO AND ALMOND KULFI

SHRIKHAND WITH FRUIT

REALLY EASY!

A creamy mixture of curd cheese and yogurt, delicately flavoured with cardamom and then mixed with a selection of fruits. You can use any fruits that are in season such as apricots, pears, papaya, guava, melon and so on.

Serves 6
500g (1 lb) curd cheese
340g (12 oz) carton thick Greek yogurt
90g (3 oz) sieved icing sugar
½ teaspoon ground cardamom
1 small mango, chopped
1 firm banana, chopped and mixed with 1 teaspoon lemon juice
60g (2 oz) seedless grapes
30g (1 oz) blanched almonds, sliced
a few fresh mint leaves

1 Put the curd cheese and yogurt into a bowl and beat together until smooth. Stir in the icing sugar and cardamom.

2 Carefully stir in the fruit. Put mixture in serving dishes. Chill and then serve decorated with almond slices and fresh mint leaves.

INDEX